Staff Orientation
in Early Childhood Programs

Barbara O'Sullivan

Toys 'n Things Press
St. Paul, Minnesota

ACKNOWLEDGMENTS

Thank you to all the hard working advocates who
are committed to young children's issues.

Barbara O'Sullivan
Spring 1990

Photography: Mike Long

Originally produced and published through funding by the Bush Foundation through a
grant to Resources for Child Caring, to promote accreditation by the National Academy of
Early Childhood Programs.

Published by: Toys 'n Things Press
                  450 North Syndicate, Suite 5
                  St. Paul, Minnesota 55104

Distributed by: Gryphon House
                  PO Box 275
                  Mt. Rainier, Maryland 20712

ISBN: 0-934140-42-1

Printed in the United States of America.

CONTENTS

Introduction 5

Welcome 9

Staff and Child Interactions 13

Observing and Recording Behavior 27

Special Needs 35

Parent and Staff Interaction 41

Curriculum 49

The Environment...59

Health, Safety and Nutrition...............................71

Team Building 91

Taking Care of Yourself 101

Evaluation and Training Plan 109

Introduction

INTRODUCTION

Working with young children is a rewarding experience. It is a chance for challenges and accomplishments. The best teachers of young children are warm, loving and enthusiastic, using their own initiative and creativity. In addition, staff members need specific training in early childhood education in order to provide valuable learning experiences for children. Research has provided us with the knowledge of an appropriate developmental model for the care of young children. Unless this research is passed on to those who work directly with young children, it is useless.

This staff orientation manual is an overview of the expectations of the position as a teacher of young children. It provides an opportunity to work with the supervisor to identify areas where additional training is needed. Contents of this manual are based on the criteria of the Accreditation system of the National Academy of Early Childhood Programs, a division of the National Association for the Education of Young Children (NAEYC). The Academy has proven successful in evaluating the components of quality in programs for young children.

HOW TO USE THIS MANUAL

The purpose of this manual is twofold: to provide ideas and skill building tools and to be a resource. Each section in the manual provides activities for involvement. For adults, as for children, learning needs to be exploratory, stimulating and fun. The handbook allows the individual to work with a page, a section or a particular problem. It can be used in new staff orientation or as a refresher for personnel already on staff. Opportunities are also provided to set goals and to design a training plan for further professional development. Specific activities are well suited to be used at staff meetings.

The manual is not a comprehensive training guide nor is it to be followed step-by-step. Personalize and individualize the orientation by substituting or adding materials relevant to your program. Consider your interests, the program's focus, your training level and experience. Photocopy the outlined forms to have as a record of each staff member's orientation. Make this a resource workable for you.

THE ORIENTATION

Staff orientation to the program should be the responsibility of an experienced staff member. Often the director takes this role, but in most programs the overwhelming job responsibilities of the director can interfere, making it necessary to designate another staff as the trainer or "mentor." Staff may be more comfortable in a peer relationship. Choosing a mentor needs to be done with care. A mentor needs both practical and theoretical knowledge. Most important is the person's attitude toward children. Modeling the behavior of an outstanding teacher can be a powerful learning tool for new staff. By ensuring consistency in staff behavior, children gain a clear perception of standards and expectations, and the assurance that everyone will be treated with understanding and respect.

The role of a mentor in orienting staff is a motivating experience. This role provides a challenge for experienced staff. This person needs to be rewarded with praise and recognition. Release time and an extra monetary bonus should also be considered.

Providing an orientation program for a new staff person will reinforce his or her choice of this job as a good one. Hopefully, the orientation program will continue to be a growing experience as we strive to provide a quality experience for the young children in our care.

STAFF ORIENTATION PLAN

Employee's Name _____

Supervisor/Mentor _____

Starting Date _____

Orientation Schedule

Date & Meeting Time   Topics

_____(Employee's Name) has completed an

orientation to _____(Program Name) on _____(date).

_____
(Employee)   (date)

_____
(Supervisor/Mentor)   (date)

_____
(Director)   (date)

Welcome

THE FIRST DAY

WELCOME! A new job is exciting and challenging. The first day of a new job can be overwhelming. There is so much to find out and many new people to meet. The "nitty gritty" are outlined along with suggestions for a smooth transition into your new job.

Jot down notes and questions for later review.

BUILDING TOUR

- children's indoor space
- kitchen
- storage areas
- resource room
- fire exits
- rest rooms for adults and children

- playground areas
- lunchroom
- staff lounge
-
-
-

Suggestions: Find out names of other organizations or groups who may also use the building. Are certain areas restricted during certain times (lunch room hours, staff lounge, etc.)? Who is responsible for opening and closing the building? Even if you are not in charge, an emergency might arise when you may be the first to arrive or the last to leave. How would you handle this situation?

PROGRAM POLICIES AND PROCEDURES

How do I...
- report for work? (time clock, sign-in sheet, report to main office)
- request personal leave or vacation?
- requisition purchase of special materials?

Whom do I notify if I am ill and unable to come to work?

What are the policies on...
- personal phone calls
- dress code

When do I get paid?

When are staff meetings?

Whom do I call on when I need to leave the room?

List additional questions. As you proceed through the manual and become better acquainted with the program, your list of questions will grow.

PERSONNEL POLICIES

Job Description
Review your job description. Note your role and responsibilities. List additional tasks you are expected to do as part of your position (e.g. order movies for children every other Friday).

Policies
State your benefits and rights as an employee of this particular program. Be sure to clarify:
* compensation and salary scales
* overtime policy
* raises and bonuses
* resignation and termination
* benefits: personal/vacation leave, sick leave
  medical and dental insurance
  maternity/paternity leave, retirement plan
  holidays, jury duty, tuition discount for your own child
* grievance procedures
* non-discriminating hiring practices
* probationary employment period
* liability insurance for staff and children
* attendance at board and/or staff meetings
* evaluation
* program philosophy for the care and education of young children

---

My job description and personnel policies have been reviewed with me.

_____

(Employee)   (date)

_____

(Supervisor/Mentor)   (date)

STAFF FILES

Your file is confidential and accessible to you at all times. Your supervisor and the state licensing examiner are the only other people who should have access to your file. Your file needs to include the following information. It is your responsibility to keep the information updated according to licensing requirements.

- Application form
- Written references
- Personnel form
- W-4 form
- Health/medical form
- Emergency form
- First aid certificate
- Inservice training record
-
-
-
-

The above information is updated and on file.

_____   _____
(Employee)   (date)

_____   _____
(Supervisor/Mentor)   (date)

Staff and Child Interaction

THE DEVELOPING CHILD

Staff who work with young children are committed to the importance of quality care and education. The National Academy of Early Childhood Programs cite interactions among staff and children as one of the major components of the Accreditation system.

Quality child care ensures that the physical, intellectual, social and emotional needs of children are met. An understanding of the developmental stages through which a child progresses makes your role clearer.

Each child who comes into group care is unique with individual needs. Genetic makeup, heredity, environmental influences, and cultural differences greatly affect the child's adjustment to the early childhood program. A child who has had many social experiences with families, friends and neighbors will most likely adjust more easily to group care than a child who has not had much exposure to social interactions. Cooperation and open communication enable the parent and caregiver to effectively work together in helping the child make a smooth transition from the home to the group child care situation.

The following section is an overview of the developmental stages of young children from birth through age seven. The concern is for the total development of the young child as a whole person. A balanced and integrated program meets the needs of the group as well as the individual child. Children develop at different rates. Therefore, it is important to be aware of the stages the child has accomplished, what the child is currently developing and to plan ahead for the next stage. With this knowledge, you will be able to interact with the child in a warm and responsive way, ensuring his or her optimal development.

BASIC PRINCIPLES OF CHILD DEVELOPMENT

1. Development occurs in a number of different areas at the same time.

2. Development is sequential.

3. One area of development affects another.

4. Children have individual rates of development.

5. Development moves from simple to complex.

6. Individual development depends on both inherited characteristics and environmental experiences.

7. Development is considered to occur in stages.

8. Development is a combination of maturation and learning.

9. Each child has an individual learning style.

SPECIAL CONSIDERATIONS FOR INFANT NEEDS

The infant caregiver should be an individual who:

- Has a sincere commitment to the infant's well-being.
- Accurately interprets infant's needs and responds promptly, appropriately, and tenderly.
- Communicates positively through body language, tone of voice, and eye contact.
- Fosters a secure attachment between the infant and self, providing infant with emotional security and freedom to explore.
- Encourages language learning from the earliest interactions through attention to communication, language games, songs, naming objects, etc.
- Is dependable, so the baby will learn trust.
- Actively observes the infant's development and shares this information with the child's parents.

IMPORTANCE OF ONE-ON-ONE INTERACTION

Planning a special infant/caregiver interaction time into the curriculum is important for several reasons:

1. It gives both the infant and caregiver an opportunity to concentrate on one another, to learn each other's rhythms, and ways of doing things. The richer the infant's experiences during this special time with the primary caregiver the more secure and able to learn the child will be when playing alone or when in a group.

2. The caregiver will, on a regular basis, be able to assess at which level of development the infant is responding, and will be better able to plan group times and interest centers to fit each infant's individual needs.

3. The infant can learn and practice new skills with special support from the caregiver but without the distractions of others. The sense of mastery will give the infant confidence to participate in group play or activity, as well as the initiative to work on similar activities on his or her own.

It is ideal for the infant and caregiver to have this special one-on-one time in a separate room away from other distractions. As the baby gets better at concentrating on various activities the sessions can be moved to where there are more distractions. Plan these activities based on the stage of development the child is at.

Chart each developmental step and plan ahead how to nourish each skill as it appears.

SPECIAL CONSIDERATIONS FOR TODDLER/PRESCHOOL NEEDS

Toddlers and preschoolers need caregivers who:

- Will help them become more self-sufficient and responsible by encouraging them to explore and discover individual abilities.

- Understand young children's tendencies to assert themselves, reject or ignore adult suggestions, and test limits.

- View negative behaviors (hitting, biting, etc) as opportunities to help children learn self-control and alternative behaviors.

- Model and reward appropriate behavior throughout the day, making sure each child is recognized.

- Understand children's need to use their whole bodies in learning and provide suitable activities and opportunities for this.

- Understand that, at this stage, the process of learning is more important than the product.

- Are able to talk with, listen to and encourage the child's language development.

- Recognize the need for social interaction with a group, time alone with a teacher, and private time.

- Recognize and appreciate each child as an individual with strengths and weaknesses.

- Realize that each child may learn in a different way, and provide a variety of learning experiences so all children have opportunities for success.

SPECIAL CONSIDERATIONS FOR SCHOOL-AGERS' NEEDS

School-agers need caregivers who:

- Recognize that much of the school-agers' out-of-school tasks are to develop resourcefulness, responsibility, and reliability.

- Remember that after three to seven hours in an academic setting, often with highly structured time and environment, school-agers need lots of opportunities for physical activities, a chance to "just play" with peers, and a chance to express themselves through open ended creative activities.

- Understand the school-ager's need for an unstructured, home-like setting; one in which they feel secure and can relax after an intense day at school. If possible, furnish an area with bean-bag chairs, a couch, large pillows, card table, shelves, etc.

- Understand how children this age grow and develop and will use this knowledge to provide school-agers' with appropriate games and activities.

- Recognize their own importance as role models in the formation of the school-ager's attitudes, values and self-image.

- Recognize that each child is unique, comes from his or her own unique background, and anticipates his or her own unique future, be it at home that evening or as an adult.

- Are able to support, direct, guide and encourage the school-ager's curiosity and need to explore and experiment, yet be able to leave the child in control so that each child can explore, reflect, expand, and complete according to his or her own rhythm and interest.

WORKSHEET

Child Development Knowledge in Practice

Spend at least two hours observing a group in your center or preschool. Using the information provided on child development, note how the teacher integrates child development knowledge into the curriculum and throughout daily interactions with the children.

Date _____ Time of observation _____

Ages of children observed _____

ACTIVITIES

(Example: Cutting out paper strips

PURPOSE

Develop fine motor skills and hand-eye coordination)

Focusing on the age group of the children you are caring for, answer the following questions:

Developmental Stages

1. What are the child's needs at this age? What messages do we need to give this child?

2. What kind of play would this child enjoy? What things would a child this age enjoy playing with?

3. What statements would this child make to sum up his or her view of the world?

4. What fears might this child have?

5. What would make this child feel happy?

6. Developmentally, what is the most important accomplishment a child makes at this stage?

SELF-ESTEEM

Three major factors determine how self-concept is formed:

1. **How children are treated.** Initially a child's personality and self-concept develop from how they are treated by others. A child perceives his or her own value from others. Most of the time, people live up or down to what other important people expect of them.

2. **Children's perception of how their family is viewed.** Great care needs to be taken to avoid thoughtless comments, that devalue parents. Respect for diversity on racial, ethnic, religious, and economic backgrounds must be shown and valued. Stereotypical responses need to be eliminated.

3. **Life experiences with success and failure.** A child care worker needs to help a child gain competence and confidence in his or her abilities so the child will feel successful.

Suggestions for Building Self-Esteem

1. Set a good example.
2. Let children know they are loved and wanted.
3. Include children in activities, decision making and problem solving.
4. Tell children their strengths.
5. Treat child with honesty and respect. Do not compare one child to another.
6. Do not make fun of children's attempts to do or understand things.
7. Avoid belittling, sarcasm, labeling, and shame.
8. Be sensitive and responsive to needs.
9. Be aware of your feelings about each child.
10. Encourage children to gain competence.
11. Praise achievements.
12. Show understanding.
13. Direct discipline towards behavior.
14. Encourage, support independence.
15. Appreciate feelings.
16. Talk with the child, not at or to him.
17. Look for opportunities for success.
18. Reward child with statements and actions just because she exists.

From *Starting Points,* Resources for Child Caring, Minnesota Child Care Training Project.

Messages to Build Self-Esteem

Using the suggestions sheet on building self-esteem, list ways to let children know they are valued. List specific words, gestures and activities to promote a positive self-concept.

Examples:

- "I'm glad to see you!," "Thanks for cleaning up," "I like your smile."
- Hugs
- OK signal
- Star of the week — each week a child posts her picture on a bulletin board with pictures of her family, drawings, etc. The child gets to be a special helper for that week as well.
- Songs and fingerplays using children's names.

At the end of today, think about what you did to promote a positive self-concept for each child in your care. You show children you care about them through your attention and the time you spend with them.

The three things I think are most important to building self-esteem in young children are:

1.

2.

3.

Something I learned about myself is:

A new idea I am going to try is:

BEHAVIOR MANAGEMENT

The word discipline is derived from the Latin which means "to teach." Positive techniques are used to help young children learn appropriate behavior. Based on our knowledge of child development, we no longer think of discipline as "punishment for being bad."

Your responsibility as a teacher is to *guide* children in learning appropriate behaviors based on their developmental level. Children want to succeed. By ensuring successful experiences for children, we will be helping them develop a healthy self-esteem as well.

Guidelines for Proactive Behavior Management

I.   Establish appropriate expectations
1.   Use developmental checklists as guides.
2.   Use your knowledge of child development and what you know are important skills for later life development.
3.   Look at frequency and intensity of behavior.
4.   Ask if it is important to me.

II.   Use differential attention
Giving attention
Step 1. Choose the kind of attention that is rewarding.
Step 2. Put variety in your attention.
Step 3.Use specific, descriptive praise.
Planned ignoring
Step 1. Ignore immediately.
Step 2. Make ignoring obvious.
Step 3. Be consistent.

III.   Catch them being good
1.   Pinpoint desirable behavior.
2.   Select a reinforcer.
3.   Be immediate.
4.   Be obvious.
5.   Be consistent and frequent.

IV.   Give effective instructions
1.   Get child's attention—use name.
2.   Keep it simple.
3.   Be clear.
4.   Set time limit.

V. What to do after an instruction.

If the behavior occurs:

    1. Give reinforcers.

    2. Give next part of instructions.

    3. Give extra reasons and comments.

If the behavior does not occur:

    1. Wait about 10 minutes without saying anything.

    2. Repeat instruction and model.

    3. Prompt behavior.

    4. Ignore negative behavior.

    5. Wait for stated time limit before providing consequence.

When All Else Fails

Time Out

1. Remember that time out will not teach appropriate behavior. It will merely teach the child what to do, rather than teaching the positive alternative.

2. You must decide if time out from a situation actually will remove reinforcers for the inappropriate behavior.

Pinpoint misbehavior

Determine length of time (2-5 minutes after child has quieted down).

Explain time out behavior procedure ahead of time.

1. Carry out procedure each time the misbehavior occurs.

2. Start time out as soon as possible.

3. Identify behavior.

4. Do not nag, scold, give explanations.

5. Ignore all protests.

6. Do not let child escape time out.

7. Use timer or a clock.

8. Add more time if misbehavior occurs during time out.

9. Reinforce good behavior in between time outs.

10. Use time out for misbehavior you have selected — use other consequences for other misbehaviors.

11. Remain calm and matter of fact.

From *Behavior Management Curriculum,* Child Care Resource and Referral, Inc., Debra Larsson, Minnesota Child Care Training Project

WHAT'S THE WORST?

The behaviors listed are commonly encountered when working with young children.

Rank in order which behaviors, in your opinion, are least tolerable. Determine your ranking based on the developmental level of most of the children in your care as well as your own tolerance of certain behaviors. This exercise is recommended for a team to see most clearly if the teachers all see behaviors in the same way. The results provide a means of "assigning" certain behaviors to certain teachers.

_____ Tattling

_____ Whining

_____ Spitting

_____ Biting

_____ Swearing

_____ Destroying other people's property

_____ Name calling

_____ Clowning around

_____ Tracking in messy shoes

_____ Clinging

_____ Not paying attention at group

_____ Fighting over toys

_____ Leaving the room without permission

(Employee)   (date)

(Supervisor/Mentor)   (date)

From *Starting Points*, Resources for Child Caring, Minnesota Child Care Training Project

SETTING GOALS

By practicing stating positive goals it will be easier to think of behavior as a learning objective for young children rather than being "good" or "bad."

Write a positive goal for each inappropriate behavior.

Tattling_____

Whining _____

Spitting _____

Biting_____

Swearing _____

Destroying other people's property _____

Name calling_____

Clowning around _____

Tracking in messy shoes _____

Clinging_____

Not paying attention at group_____

Fighting over toys_____

Leaving the room without permission_____

Examples are given for stating positive goals for inappropriate behaviors.

Behavior	Goal
Biting	Sharing toys with other children
Tantrum	Using words for what you want
Running in the room	Walking
Eating with fingers	Using a fork to eat with

_____

(Employee)   (date)

_____

(Supervisor/Mentor)   (date)

From Debra Larsson, *Managing Children's Behavior....Proactively*, Child Care Resource and Referral, Inc., Minnesota Child Care Training Project.

BEHAVIORAL MANAGEMENT PLAN

Using the **Guidelines for Proactive Behavior Management**, outline a plan staff will use for the top 3 behaviors ranked as worst. Remember: time out is the last resort.

1.

2.

3.

How does this behavior management approach differ from how you were raised by your own parents or guardians?

_____

(Employee)   (date)

_____

(Supervisor/Mentor)   (date)

Behavior Management — Summary

1. Behavior management teaches desirable behaviors. It teaches positive adaptive alternatives for undesirable behaviors.

2. Interaction between adult and child is positive, producing less stress for the adult and child. It's difficult to remain calm while trying to lecture or reason with a child who does not want to listen to a recap of the bad behavior the child is already so aware of.

3. The adult models values and expectations for the child. Proactive management demonstrates non-aggressive ways to let someone know you don't like something they've done.

4. Proactive management gives lots of opportunities for praise and attention which build healthy self-esteem.

5. Pleasant and healthy relationships develop between the adult and the child.

6. Behavior management prevents problems from occurring. It helps the child sooner, before a problem develops.

From Debra Larsson, *Managing Children's Behavior....Proactively*, Child Care Resource and Referral, Inc., Minnesota Child Care Training Project.

Resources:

Clarke, Jean, *Self-esteem: A Family Affair.*

Kraus, R., *Leo the Late Bloomer.*

Toys 'n Things Press, *Communicate Awareness Posters*:
  Use More Do's Than Don'ts
  Use Kind Words
  Communicate Acceptance
  Give the Child Plenty of Praise

Briggs, Dorothy, *Your Child's Self-esteem.*

Crary, Elizabeth, *Without Spanking or Spoiling.*

Crary, Elizabeth, *Children's Problem Solving Books: I Can't Wait; I Want It; I Want to Play;* and *My Name is not Dummy.*

Parent's Magazine Films, *Dealing with Daily Situations,* a set of five filmstrips and cassettes from the series *Working With Children: A Commitment to Caring.*

Recordings:

Palmer, Hap. *Getting to Know Myself.*

Thomas, Marlo. *Free to Be...You and Me.*

Observing and
Recording Behavior

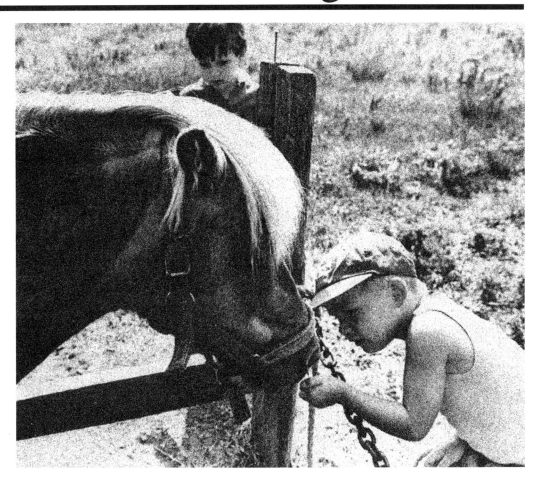

OBSERVING AND RECORDING BEHAVIOR

Observing and keeping records of children's behavior is a way to gain insight into what they do, why they do it, and how they change over a period of time. By knowing more about a child, you can better provide experiences that will meet the needs of that particular child and will help you expand the child's interest.

Descriptive and objective observations can be used to:

- **Identify** the source of a problem (not just the individual child but also the environment and the other children with whom he or she associates).

- **Gain** a better understanding of the child's skill level, behavior, purposes and feelings.

- **Observe** repeatedly over a period of time to show how a child's development is progressing.

- **Show** how a child's development is progressing.

- **Provide** examples when discussing a child's progress with his or her parents.

It is important that parents be aware of any concerns you have. Involve parents in the planning you do for their child. Most parents will appreciate the sharing of information. Discuss the *objective* information you gather in your recorded observations, add *subjective* information that you interpret from the observations.

Observation Tips

- Sit, look and listen.

- Observe and record verbalizations as well as nonverbal behavior including voice tone, postures, gestures, mannerisms and facial expressions.

- Be unobtrusive.

- Do not interact any more than usual with the child you are observing.

- Be objective.

- Use descriptive words to define the behavior.

- Do interpret emotions such as angry, sad, afraid.

- Be honest about your own personal values and biases.

Considerations for Observations

It is impossible to observe everything a child does. Therefore, it is important to determine beforehand the specific behavior you want to observe, while trying to remain open to the unexpected or other information. Following are some general questions to keep in mind when observing young children. Reading these questions over several times before you begin your observation will help you remember what to look for.

1. What is the specific situation in which the child is operating?
   (What other activities are going on? What are the general expectations of the group at the moment and what is the general atmosphere of the room — noisy, calm, boisterous, quiet?)

2. What is the child's approach to materials and activities?
   (Is the child slow in getting started or does he plunge right in? Does the child use materials in the usual way or does he use them in different ways, exploring them for the possibilities they offer?)

3. How interested is the child in what he is doing?
   (Does he seem intent on what he is doing or does the child seem more interested in what others are doing? How long is the child's concentration span? How often does he shift activities?)

4. How much energy does the child use?
   (Does he work at a fairly even pace or does he work in "spurts" of activity? Does he use a great deal of energy in manipulating the materials, in body movements or in talking?)

5. What are the child's body movements like?
   (Does the child's body seem tense or relaxed? Are his movements jerky, uncertain or poorly coordinated?)

6. What does the child say?
   (Does the child talk, sing, hum or use nonsense words while he works? Does he use sentences, single words? How does the child communicate with others — words or gestures?)

7. What is the child's affect?
   (What are his facial expressions like? Does he appear frustrated?)

8. How does the child get along with other children?
   (Does he play alone, with only certain children, or with a variety of children? Willing or unwilling to share toys? Does he initiate or follow along with group ideas?)

9. What kinds of changes are there between the beginning and the end of an activity?
   (Does the child's mood change as he works?)

10. What is the child's relationship with you?
    (Is the child eager to see you when he comes to tell you about what he is doing?)

11. What is the child's relationship with his parents?
    (Is the child eager to see them at the end of the day? Does the child share with them the things he has been doing?)

From *Starting Points*, Resources for Child Caring, Minnesota Child Care Training Project.

RECORDING TECHNIQUES

Time Sampling Method

The following is an example of a time sampling method of recording. Every half hour write down what the child is doing at that moment. You may want to think of this as snapping a picture every one-half hour — what do you see? This record of the child's activities will help you to learn more about what the child does during the day.

Below is a sample of a daily activities record.

7:30 a.m.   Standing near door, mother taking off snowsuit, John crying.

8:00 a.m.   Sitting at table, eating dry cereal with fingers, babbling to self, watching baby across the table.

8:30 a.m.   Sitting on floor close to Joan, but not looking at her, putting blocks in and out of can, smiling as blocks go in, uses both hands with steady grip.

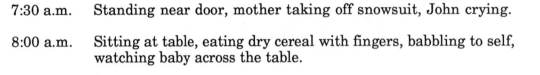

Choose a child and use a time sampling method for recording. Remember: describe behavior in descriptive terms.

_____

(Employee)   (date)

_____

(Supervisor/Mentor)   (date)

From *Starting Points*, Resources for Child Caring, Minnesota Child Care Training Project.

Diary Record

A diary record is a detailed account of what a child does for a specific period of time. To do a diary record, write down everything the child you are observing says or does, everything other children say or do with the child and everything you say or do with him.

Select a time when you can observe uninterrupted for at least 15 minutes. Do not set up anything special for the children. Just try to observe the child doing the kinds of things he usually does.

It is important that you sit where you can see or hear well and can observe without drawing the child's attention to what you are doing. (If the children do become aware of your observation and ask questions, tell them what you are doing and why. Do not identify a specific child, but rather state that you are observing the children in general. ("I am watching all of you play.")

1. Time observation started _____

2. Briefly describe the situation as you begin.

What is the child doing?

Where is the child?

Who else is near the child?

What else is going on?

_____   _____
(Employee)   (date)

_____   _____
(Supervisor/Mentor)   (date)

From *Starting Points*, Resources for Child Caring, Minnesota Child Care Training Project.

Developmental Checklist

A checklist is another tool which can be used to record the skills of one child or a group of children. This tool assists in identifying at what level a child is performing a particular skill and what he has yet to accomplish. Begin by determining the sequence of skill development and designing a graph. Then arrange for an opportunity for the child or children to perform the task. As you observe, check the items you see the child or children perform. The following is an example of a checklist of an individual's skills at using a scissor.

EXAMPLE: SKILLS

CHILD'S NAME & BIRTH DATE	Holds correctly	Snips	Fringes	Cuts corners off	Cuts curves freehand	Cuts in on alley	Cuts on thick lines	Cuts on narrow lines
Bill 12/31/83	X	X	X	X				
Tara 3/30/83	X	X						
Shawn 8/23/83	X							
Josh 3/10/84	X	X	X	X	X			

The checklist is also a valuable tool for listing a number of different skills you would like to see a child or group of children learn during a given period of time. List some of the goals you have. Then organize activities in which you will see the child or children porform the task. When it is apparent that the child is able to consistently perform the skill, check or date the appropriate column to indicate the child has completed the goal.

EXAMPLE: MOTOR

CHILD'S NAME & BIRTH DATE	Runs smoothly	Walks upstairs alternating feet	Throws ball	Catches ball	Dresses self			
Thea 10/31/83	X	X	X	X	X			
Katie 9/30/83			X	X	X			
Ben 8/15/83	X	X	X	X	X			
Gina 1/5/84	X		X					
Lisa 3/11/84			X					

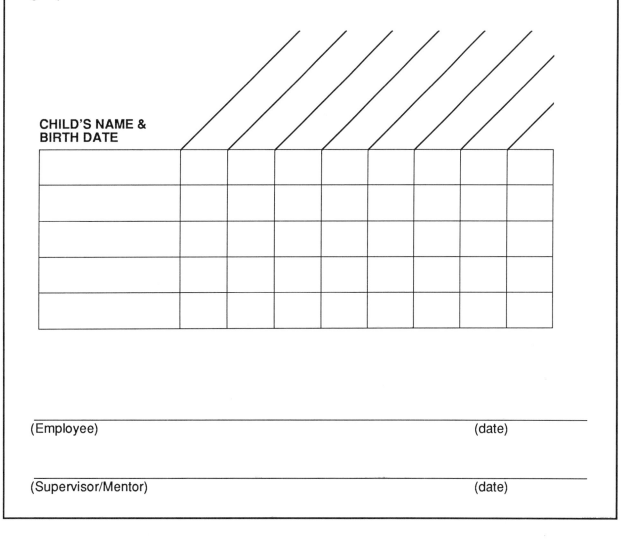

Developmental Checklist

Refer to the developmental chart for the physical skills of the age group of children with whom you are working. List the specific skills you want to track for development. Choose five children in your group and record their skill level.

CHILD'S NAME & BIRTH DATE

_____
(Employee)   (date)

_____
(Supervisor/Mentor)   (date)

SCREENING

A formalized way of looking at a child's needs and skills is by *screening* the child's skills. Screening does not diagnose problems, measure intelligence, or predict future needs, but can:

- add information to verify observations;
- be useful in planning curriculum;
- demonstrate specific strengths and weakness depending on age;
- give information to parents and other professionals involved with the child;
- add credibility to your program.

There are many screening tools developed for these purposes. Many can be administered by child care staff. Others should only be given by professionals specifically trained in interpreting the tool. Screening can measure:

- general health
- vision and hearing
- motor development
- self help skills
- speech and language
- behavior and social skills
- learning and thinking skills

Parent permission is needed when doing formalized screening. A sample permission form is provided if your program does not have its own.

I give my permission for my child _____ (name)

to participate in testing administered by

_____

I understand the staff will select only those tests which they judge not harmful or abusive. I also understand I will be informed of the results of any test that indicates information significant to the development of my child.

Date: _____   Signed:_____
                                        (Parent or Guardian)

Resources:

Observing the Development of the Young Child, Janice Beatty

Developmental Achievement Chart for Infants and Toddlers, Inez D. Moyer

Developmental Screening in Early Childhood Education, S. Meisels

Evaluating Children's Progress, Southeastern Day Care Project

Preschool Development Inventory, Harold Treton

Teacher's Inventory of Emotional and Behavioral Development, Yale University Child Study Center

Observing and Recording the Behavior of Young Children, Dorothy H. Cohen.

Video

Looking at Young Children: Observing in Early Childhood Settings, created by the Center for Early Education and Development, University of Minnesota.

Special Needs

SPECIAL NEEDS

Every child in your care is unique with individual needs and deserves special attention. Because of a child's developmental level, family environment or health concerns, staff members need to look at ways to best meet all a child's needs. Some children have a need for an extra hug or hand; others need extra patience or understanding. Others need greater attention in special programming and services.

Whatever the special need, staff need to be:

- attentive in assessing what the needs are
- flexible in planning for them
- realistic in which children's needs can be safely and appropriately met in your setting.

Observation and Assessment of Individual Needs

To be attentive to children's individual needs it is necessary to look at your feelings about specific children and take an objective look at the situation.

When working with children with special needs, the child care staff may experience a wide assortment of emotional responses including sympathy, pity, frustration, fear, repulsion and/or anger. These feelings can affect your response to children. A response may be to overly protect a child, or it may be to focus only on a child's weaknesses rather than on strengths. Fear or insecurity may limit you in trying to meet the child's need. It is expected that you will have some or all of these feelings or responses at times. To most effectively deal with them and the children you serve is to admit or acknowledge the feeling to fellow staff who can aid you in working with the child in the most effective way.

Some children in your care may have special needs that have not been identified. You may be the only professional other than the child's physician who has had contact with the child. Sometimes child care professionals get a "hunch" about a particular child that alerts them to take a closer look at a child's functioning.

Children With Special Needs:

- Perform below what is normally expected of children their age.
- May demonstrate a delay in one or more of the following areas:
  - cognitive
  - motor (large muscle and fine motor)
  - speech/language
  - social-emotional
  - neurological
  - other related developmental area (attention span)
- May be mildly, moderately, or severely delayed.*
- May at first appear to be "age-appropriate" (does not necessarily have an obvious visible handicap).

* A significant delay is usually regarded as being a 25% delay of a child's age level. For example, a four year old with only three year old skills in communication has a one year or 25% delay.

- Have problems which interfere with their ability to learn, solve problems, communicate, move around, play with peers, or respond to discipline, etc.

- Have some strengths and some special needs. For example, a child can be socially and emotionally immature (below age level), but his language will be appropriate for his age.

- With appropriate help some children with special needs can catch up before they begin Kindergarten. Others will continue to need help.

- Need and will benefit from early intervention and early childhood education!**

- Some special needs can be noticed from birth. Intervention can begin at infancy.

** Over a period of years, research and intervention programs have shown the importance and success of working with children with special needs at an early age.

From *Caring for Special Children*, Greater Minneapolis Day Care Association.

SPECIAL TECHNIQUES

Helping the aggressive child:

1. Follow a routine for arrivals and departures.

2. Before a transition, give several reminders that the activity will be changing.

3. Encourage the child to express his feelings in words, not actions. Pick out an activity or area where child can work out anger.

4. Remind the child if he is losing control of prompt appropriate behaviors.

5. During group activities (circle, story, conversation, etc.) give the child enough personal space. Seat the child between non-aggressive children or near adults.

6. Control the child's level of stimulation by removing unused materials, slowing down activity, or introducing quiet activity.

Helping the anxious child:

1. Prepare the child for new activities by introducing the activity or area beforehand.

2. In group activities, seat the child between non-aggressive children. Encourage, but don't force participation.

3. Help the child understand that it is more important to try an activity than to do it perfectly.

4. Allow the child to work at his own pace.

5. Help the child recognize when he is becoming anxious and to seek help from adults.

Helping the hyperactive child:

1. Give short, clear and calm directions about transitions and throughout activities. Provide adult supervision.

2. Control level of excitement; remind the child when he gets too excited and ask the child to rest if he is losing control.

3. During group activities, call on the child frequently to keep his attention.

4. Use demonstrations to keep child's attention.

5. Don't expect prolonged sitting — break tasks into small segments that can be done in a short time.

6. Gradually increase the amount of time you expect the child to attend to and perform tasks.

Helping the withdrawn child:

1. Encourage and support participation, but allow the child to watch and listen.

2. Respond positively to the child's attempts to communicate in order to build self-confidence.

3. Provide the child with individual attention and instructions.

4. Gradually involve the child in a few simple activities. Introduce other children into these activities gradually.

Helping the pre-verbal child:

1. Babies cry because they have needs which need to be met.

2. These needs can erupt or change suddenly.

3. Babies have no ability to be patient so their needs should be anticipated or met promptly.

4. Basic infant needs/reasons for crying are:

   • food/hunger

   • rest/sleepiness

   • diapering/wet diaper

   • stimulation/boredom

   • health/illness or teething

These are reasons for infantile crying. If their needs are met, babies usually will not cry. Crying is a baby's tool for communication. Be aware of which need(s) a child might be expressing.

DISCUSSION QUESTIONS

1. If all young children develop at different rates, how can a child with special needs be identified for early intervention?

2. What steps should you take if you have concerns about the development of a child in your care?

3. What are some reactions you may expect from parents when approaching them about your concern for their child?

4. What are your personal feelings about including a child with special needs into your group?

    • How would the other children react?

    • What obstacles or problems do you see?

    • What additional assistance and/or information would you need?

    • What would be the benefits for all children involved?

_____   _____
(Employee)   (date)

_____   _____
(Supervisor/Mentor)   (date)

COMMUNITY RESOURCES AND REFERRALS

Review: Developmental Stages of Young Children,
            Observing and Recording Behavior
            Environment
            Parent Communication

List resources in your community which provide services for young children. Include services provided by local child care resource and referral agencies, and public health, social services and education departments of the county and state.

Agency/Organization   **Service Provided**

Resources:

Developmental Screening in Early Childhood: A Guide, S. Meisels

Including All of Us, Merle Frosche, et al.

Adapting Early Childhood Curricula, Ruth E. Cook & Virginia B. Armbruster

Resources for Teaching Young Children With Special Needs, Penny Low Deiner

Gifted Young Children, Wendy C. Roedell, et al.

Parent and Staff
Interaction

PARENT AND STAFF INTERACTIONS

Parents are the principal influence in a child's life. While it is not always easy, a partnership between parent and teacher is always worth the effort because it gives the child a support system for success in school. Set up an open communication system. Keeping in close touch with parents throughout the year helps them feel they are part of their child's care and education.

Based upon our knowledge of child development and background experiences from our own families, we value certain aspects of a child's experiences while in our care. Parents and staff may place different priorities on values. For example, parents may be very upset that there is paint on their child's clothes which will override your enthusiasm of sharing the child's beautiful painting.

You also may find differences in values among the staff. Your co-worker may insist on all children participating in group time while you may feel the child should have a choice. It is unimportant who is right or wrong; focus upon what is best for the child. Your respect for a child's parents is essential to the child's own self-esteem.

You are the professional. Part of acting professionally is being able to focus on the other person and not being caught up in your own personal feelings.

SEPARATION ISSUES

Preparing a child for what to expect upon entering a preschool program leads to a smooth transition. Even with preparation, a child may still be fearful and anxious. Staff and parents need to work together to acknowledge the child's fear and to assure a successful experience.

Activities that relieve stress of separation are:

1. Handle separations honestly. Have the parent tell the child when she is leaving and when she will return. Acknowledge a child's feelings of uncertainty, fear or anger. Provide whatever supports will be useful to the child (stuffed animal, favorite blanket, etc.). Realize that a parent's ambiguity or concern over separation may magnify a child's fears.

2. Point out familiar toys or activities. Let child proceed at his own pace. Encourage parent to stay with child until he feels comfortable and only leave for short time periods at first.

3. Have child bring an object from home or parent's possession to help bridge the gap.

4. Make a time calendar with familiar daytime activities such as playing, eating, napping, and the parent's arrival to take the child home, and let the child move the spinner as the day progresses.

5. Read children's stories dealing with separation. Have adult tell child about her own separation experience. Act out separation experiences with puppets or toy kangaroos with babies in their pouches.

6. Parents need to acknowledge their own feelings, such as guilt and sorrow about separation.

PARENT POLICIES

When parents enrolls their children in an early childhood program, they are asked to sign a contract or an agreement form. The parent agrees to follow certain policies and procedures. The program also agrees to follow certain policies and procedures. Read a copy of your program's parent contract and answer the following questions.

1. What are the program's written procedures?

2. What goals does the program set for children enrolled?

3. What is the orientation process for the children and their parents?

4. What hours does the program operate?

   a. Are there provisions for parents to bring their children earlier or pick up later?

   b. Is there a late charge?

5. What are the fees?

6. When is a child considered too ill to attend the program?

   a. Are there provisions to care for sick children at the program?

7. On which holidays does the program close?

8. What are the sign-in and sign-out procedures for parents?

_____   _____
(Employee)   (date)

_____   _____
(Supervisor/Mentor)   (date)

WORKING PARENTS

Over 60% of women with children work outside the home (National Commission on Working Women Report, 1985). However, attitudes in our society have not quite caught up with the facts. Mothers from dual career families and single parent families are often viewed as belonging in the home. In some cases, this is not even economically feasible.

1. What are your views on working mothers?

2. What do you feel the children in your care are gaining by being in child care?

3. Do you feel children would gain anything more by being home with a parent? If so, what?

4. Finish the following statements:

    I don't like it when parents...

    Parents expect too much when they ask me to..,

    I appreciate it when parents...

    I try to show appreciation for parents by...

    Parents need to know when their children...

    Parents want to know when their children...

_____

(Employee)   (date)

_____

(Supervisor/Mentor)   (date)

VALUES CLARIFICATION

Rank in order the values you feel are most important to encourage in young children.

_____	clean and neat	_____	sociability
_____	academic skills	_____	sense of humor
_____	creativity	_____	respect for adults
_____	fun-loving	_____	cooperative
_____	manners	_____	stand-up for own rights

Compare your ranking with other staff members. This ranking activity is helpful as a starting point of discussion between staff and parents. There are no right answers. The exercise will help clarify different points of view and will lead staff and parents in understanding the other's perspective.

PARENT COMMUNICATION

Direct daily contact between staff and parents is an ideal. The reality of the child care setting probably may not make this a possibility. However, other effective methods of communication can establish a good link.

- **Newsletters**: to inform parents about special activities.

- **Bulletin boards**: post schedules, lesson plans, menus, pictures of staff with names, pictures of children in the room. Note — if board becomes overloaded, parents will read nothing. Neatness counts!

- **Special notes**: individualized letters on special accomplishments of a child. Problems or concerns about a child need direct communication.

- **Alerts to illnesses**: these should be available from your public health department.

- **Phone calls**: check first with parents if they can be called at work about non-emergency matters.

- **Home visits**: real insight can be gained about a child when visited in the home setting. This is a very effective way to meet a new child enrolled in your program.

- **Journals**: some staff enjoy this, others find it burdensome. On specified days staff writes an entry for each child. Space is available for parents to leave a written response. This is an effective way to log a child's interests, activities and behavior patterns. Different staff can be assigned a list of children for a specified time period.

  Sample schedule: Children with last names beginning with letter:
  A - L — Monday & Wednesday log entries
  M - Z — Tuesday & Thursday log entries

- **Interest and needs questionnaire**: Limit questions to 4 or 5, inquiring about parent expectations for their child, the program, activities the child might enjoy at home.

- **Establish**: a parent lending library.

- **Presentations**: on topics of interest to parents such as toilet training or kindergarten readiness.

CONFIDENTIALITY

Information shared with you by parents must be held in strictest confidence. Your relationship with the parent needs to be built on mutual trust. You will probably have good relationships with 99% of the parents with whom you have contact. However, the other 1% can cause you many headaches. Sometimes the reason for this difficulty is a personality clash.

You are the professional and need to act the part. While negative feelings about a particular parent are real you cannot relay this directly to the parent. You will be told things you may not agree with. Knowing this information will help you relate better to a child. The exception to confidentiality is if there is information which leads you to believe a child is being abused and/or neglected. Then you are obligated by law to report to the specified authorities. If you are unsure about any information you receive, talk to your supervisor.

TIPS FOR EFFECTIVE PARENT CONFERENCES

- Arrange a setting that is comfortable and private for both you and the parent(s). It's best to sit informally with parents at an adult height table.

- Organize. Have notes, papers or problems needing to be presented available.

- Begin and end each conference on a positive note. In some cases, this may be hard, but it's never impossible. Think about the child's leadership qualities, sense of humor, cooperation, curiosity.

- Use specific examples, based on observations you have made about the child, (e.g., John and Sarah work together to create some wonderful building block structures).

- Listen to what the parent(s) have to say. Discuss what the parent is working on at home and build on that, (e.g., drinking from a cup, toilet training, manners, tantrums).

- Work out a plan or some goals that you and the parent agree on to use as a framework for future communication.

- If you use any type of evaluation tool, it should be covered.

- Briefly summarize the conference, indicating goals set. Keep this in the child's record.

- While it is best to converse with the parent without the child present, it may not be possible. Have materials on hand to keep the child occupied (drawing materials, books, shells, etc.).

- Schedule conferences at times most convenient for the parent. Post the schedule in advance. A reminder notice sent out ahead is often helpful to a busy parent.

SPRING AND FALL CONFERENCE

Name _____   Birthdate _____

Teachers _____   Date _____

LARGE MUSCLE DEVELOPMENT: Locomotor movement and coordination. Activities include: running, jumping, climbing, exercises, balancing & games.

Date

____ ____   ____ ____

1st Year		2nd Year		
SPR	**FALL**	**SPR**	**FALL**	
____	____	____	____	Enjoys indoor activities.
____	____	____	____	Enjoys outdoor activities.
____	____	____	____	Is developing well for age.
____	____	____	____	Movement patterns are sometimes unbalanced and out of control.
____	____	____	____	Movement patterns are consistently unbalanced and out of control.
____	____	____	____	Needs encouragement.
____	____	____	____	Sometimes overeager and loses control.
____	____	____	____	Cautious

FINE MOTOR DEVELOPMENT: Skill in handling manipulative materials. Activities include: cutting, pasting, painting, coloring puzzles, stringing, peg work and transference.

____	____	____	____	Developing well for age.
____	____	____	____	Needs assistance and practice.
____	____	____	____	Tense
____	____	____	____	Uncertain

ORGANIZED GROUP EXPERIENCE: Stories, games, group time music, finger plays and sharing.

____	____	____	____	Pays attention.
____	____	____	____	Contributes relevant ideas and information.
____	____	____	____	Participates in a variety of group activities.
____	____	____	____	Needs reminders.
____	____	____	____	Distracting to group.
____	____	____	____	Indifferent.
____	____	____	____	Hesitant
____	____	____	____	Often interrupts

WORK HABITS: Establishing a foundation of order, a good cycle of activity, concentration skills and self confidence for successful learning.

____	____	____	____	Shows self-initiative.
____	____	____	____	Confident
____	____	____	____	Proudly shares personal accomplishments.
____	____	____	____	Seeks help often.
____	____	____	____	Reluctant to try.
____	____	____	____	Easily frustrated.
____	____	____	____	Needs encouragement to choose materials.
____	____	____	____	Is easily distracted.
____	____	____	____	Chooses to work alone.
____	____	____	____	Completes a work cycle.
____	____	____	____	Detached and dreamy.
____	____	____	____	Difficulty following directions.

____ ____   ____ ____   Follows directions.

RESPECT FOR THE ENVIRONMENT:

____ ____   ____ ____   Shows care in the use of materials.
____ ____   ____ ____   Is careless with materials.
____ ____   ____ ____   Cooperates in room clean up.
____ ____   ____ ____   Frequently needs reminders to clean up.

COMMUNICATION: Listening and speaking skills.

____ ____   ____ ____   Usually listens attentively.
____ ____   ____ ____   Sometimes has difficulty listening.
____ ____   ____ ____   Clearly expresses self verbally.
____ ____   ____ ____   Difficulty being understood.

Teacher's signature _____   Date _____

From Early Childhood Directors Association, 450 N. Syndicate, Suite 5, St. Paul, MN 55104

PARENT INVOLVEMENT

The child care program provides a wonderful and necessary support system for families. The role of a child care worker is more important than ever in our society. By working closely with parents you provide a wonderful experience for young children. The key to this quality experience is maintaining open communication with parents. Parents need to be a welcome part of any early childhood program.

List below ways your parents are actively involved at your child care setting.

Examples: parent board, classroom helpers, annual conferences, volunteers for field trips.

Resources:

New Faces, New Spaces: Helping Children Cope with Change, Toys 'n Things Press.

Parents As Partners, poster and brochure series, National Association for the Education of Young Children, 1834 Connecticut Avenue NW, Washington, D.C. 20009-5786.

Stress and the Healthy Family, Dolores Curran.

Parent-Provider Communication Curriculum, Child Care Resource and Referral, Inc., Minnesota Child Care Training Project.

Curriculum

CURRICULUM

The National Academy of Early Childhood Programs advocates activities for children to be developmentally appropriate. These activities promote success for the child because they are geared to developmental stage and individual ability and interest.

Developmentally appropriate goals for young children are:

- building healthy and positive self concepts
- providing opportunities to enhance social skills
- encouraging children to think and reason, question, experiment
- promoting language development
- encouraging and demonstrating sound health, safety and nutrition habits
- respecting cultural diversity
- developing initiative and decision making skills
- providing opportunities for physical development.

THE IMPORTANCE OF PLAY

Children need years of play with real objects and events before they are ready to understand the meaning of symbols such as letters and numbers. Learning takes place as young children *touch*, *manipulate* and *experiment* with things and *interact* with people.

Children's play is the essential component of a developmentally appropriate curriculum. The important point is to choose an appropriate curriculum which considers the process of learning rather then the product.

The curriculum needs to routinely encourage the expression of social and emotional issues. The hopes, fears, anger, joys and friendships of children need to be explored. In designing a curriculum, the personal interests of the children must be capitalized on: a new baby, a visit from grandmother, dinosaurs, friends or a birthday. Program components (dramatic play, art, music, etc.) need to relate to events and interests in the children's lives.

DEVELOPMENTALLY APPROPRIATE GOALS

For each goal, give examples how the needs of children in your group are met. Use examples from your lesson plans, daily activities, the physical environment and interactions of staff with children. Review the developmental chart for your age group.

- self-concept

- social skills

- think
- reason
- question
- experiment

- language

- health

- safety

- nutrition

- cultural diversity

- initiative

- decision making

- physical

_____
(Employee)   (date)

_____
(Supervisor/Mentor)   (date)

THE DAILY SCHEDULE

A quality early childhood program provides activities that are stimulating and challenging to young children. A good program also provides a routine and consistency which offers security to young children.

Toddler/Preschool Schedule Guidelines

Each group will need to establish a routine which provides for consistent, yet flexible care that is adaptable to the changing needs of the children. Strive for:

- a balance of active and less active time.

- alternate periods of noisy and quiet activities.

- group activities and individual activities.

- open and realistic provisions for toileting.

- lunch and snack times which respond to individual patterns of eating, are relaxed and provide for social interaction between the children and the children and staff. (Teacher should eat with the group).

- designated nap and rest times to fit needs. Some toddlers may need a nap period in the forenoon and a two-hour block of time should be set aside every afternoon for sleeping or resting by everyone.

- opportunities every day for both outdoor and indoor gross motor activities.

- opportunities every day for small motor skill practice.

- language skills development integrated into all other activities.

- specific transition time activities. (Transition times are the most likely times for behavior problems, since children don't like having to stop an activity they are interested in nor do they have much patience for waiting.)

School-Age Schedule Guidelines

- Plan activities that can be self-selected and self-initiated.

- Take advantage of the mixed-age groupings which, much like in average neighborhood settings, the younger children can learn from the older ones and the older ones can learn from instructing the younger ones.

- Avoid letting this time become an extension of the highly structured school day. If a child, however, chooses to do homework he or she should be supported in that effort.

- Provide a range of activities for the children to choose from or allow them to choose to do nothing. The activity choices should include: outdoor play and/or large motor indoor activities, arts and crafts, cooking, self help skills, dramatic play, construction/woodworking, the natural sciences, hobbies, music and dancing, puzzles, board and card games.

- Stress games that are non-competitive in nature or which encourage the child to become self-challenging.

- Create a setting where children will cooperate in housekeeping chores. Being included in helping makes the center a home-like place that is theirs.

SCHEDULE EVALUATION

Evaluate your group's daily schedule and give examples of how a balance is provided for:

• active/quiet play

• teacher directed/child initiated

• structured/free play

• large group/small group/individual activities

_____   _____

(Employee)   (date)

_____   _____

(Supervisor/Mentor)   (date)

SCHEDULE FOR TODAY

Day _____ Teacher _____ Assistant _____

I. Large Group (songs, topic discussion, language: stories)

II. Play Period/Art Choices

Easel: _____   Manipulatives/Toy Table _____

Table 1 _____   Science Focus _____

Table 2 _____   Monthly Creative Dramatic Focus _____

_____

Table 3 _____   Library/Readiness Center _____

Family Living Center _____

Large Muscle Room (circle)

1. Climber   7. Blocks, Large Hollow
2. Sand Table   8. Blocks, Small Wooden
3. Water Table   9. Matt
4. Bean Bags   10. Vehicles
5. Woodwork Bench   11. Other _____
6. Balance Beam

III. Small Group (Topics and/or Activities)

1. _____
2. _____
3. _____

IV. Movement (circle)

A. Creative Movement   B. Outdoor Play (Dress for the weather)
   Instruments   Indoor Play (Gym or Classroom)
   Dance/Rhythm
   Exercise/Tumbling
   Marching

From Faye Rautio, Coordinator; Independent School District 281, Creative Play Program, Robbinsdale Area Schools

LESSON PLANNING

1. A good lesson plan provides:
   - goals for the group
   - goals for individual children
   - activities as methods to achieve goals
   - materials needed
   - appropriate activities for learners
   - activities and visuals which demonstrate cultural, religious and nonsexist acceptance.

2. Consider motivational strategies:
   - set the scene
   - share information
   - ask questions
   - encourage experimentation

3. Prepare a lesson plan for next week including the following areas:
   - language experience
   - spacial relations
   - peer relations
   - sensory activities
   - motor activities
   - imitation games
   - individualized activities

   List objectives, skills to develop, activity or procedure.

   Example: Goal—to develop spacial relation concepts
   Activity—Obstacle Course
   Objectives—
   1. to reinforce over, under, through language
   2. to follow directions-imitation
   3. to develop large motor skills
   4. to encourage group involvement-peer relations

_____

(Employee)   (date)

_____

(Supervisor/Mentor)   (date)

```
┌─────────────────────────────────────────────────────────────┐
│                                                               │
│                  LESSON PLAN WORKSHEET                         │
│                                                               │
│   1. What is the theme or general focus?                      │
│                                                               │
│                                                               │
│                                                               │
│                                                               │
│   2. What are the objectives for this lesson?                 │
│                                                               │
│                                                               │
│                                                               │
│                                                               │
│   3. What activities or procedures will be used?             │
│                                                               │
│                                                               │
│                                                               │
│                                                               │
│   4. What skills will children develop?                       │
│                                                               │
│                                                               │
│                                                               │
│                                                               │
└─────────────────────────────────────────────────────────────┘
```

Resources:

There are an abundance of books on planning activities for infants, toddlers, preschoolers and school age children. Some are excellent, some are not.

Use the following criteria for evaluating curricula and activities:

- fosters creativity
- respects cultural diversity
- activities are developmentally appropriate
- encourages thinking and reasoning skills
- allows for individual space
- incorporates the child's immediate world
- descriptive but not prescriptive: can be interrelated with other curriculum and activities

Recommended Readings:

Active Learning for Infants, D. Cryer, T. Harms, B. Bourland.

Developmentally Appropriate Practice, Sue Bredekamp, Editor, NAEYC.

Toddler Day Care, Robin Leavitt & Brenda Eheart.

Resources for Creative Teaching in Early Childhood Education, Bonnie M. Flemming & Darlene S. Hamilton.

Half A Childhood (School-Age Child Care), J. Blender, B. Schwlyer-Hass Elder, C.H.Flatter.

ATTITUDE SURVEY

It's the Little Things That Count

This activity can be used individually or as a discussion starter with staff. It will help staff clarify their values about the necessity of routine and defined procedures.

INSTRUCTIONS: The statements listed represent some common attitudes about routines and procedures. Read each statement and indicate where on the continuum you stand.

1. Children should line up to go from one room to another during a change in activities.

x _____ x

strongly disagree   strongly agree

2. There usually has to be a set period of time for using the bathroom.

x _____ x

strongly disagree   strongly agree

3. Boys and girls should use the same bathroom.

x _____ x

strongly disagree   strongly agree

4. Children should have snack when they feel like it.

x _____ x

strongly disagree   strongly agree

5. Children who don't want to listen to story or take part in group should be allowed to do as they wish as long as it does not disturb others.

x _____ x

strongly disagree   strongly agree

From *Starting Points*, Resources for Child Caring, Minnesota Child Care Training Project.

TRANSITIONS

Moving a Group Through Transitions

The transitions involved in moving from one activity to another can sometimes be difficult for children. Problems can occur because children come to activity closure at varying rates. A few children are able to complete an activity within minutes, and others lag behind in finishing their projects. Those who finish first need to have clear messages and expectations about what they are to do as they wait. Appropriate activities during transition times can also be helpful in decreasing inappropriate behavior that sometimes takes place.

The following suggestions may help smooth out the rough edges in your day:

1. Have an established procedure and follow it consistently — for example, after clean-up, take books and sit on the rug, or come to the piano. Allow ample time to get routine established. Give children warnings about when changes in activities are coming, e.g., "In two minutes it will be time to clean up."

2. Avoid having children wait in line unoccupied for handwashing, toileting or any activity. Use time as teachable moments. Review the day's accomplishments, remind them of what's coming next, reflect on children's strengths. Have a few children go at a time while the group as a whole is occupied.

3. Use easily interrupted transitional activities. Examples: send small groups of children for handwashing, toileting, etc., without disturbing the other children's concentration. Finger plays, exercising, singing, sharing time, conversation and looking at individual books are good transitional activities. A group storytime is not as good since it is not desirable to interrupt children listening to stories.

4. Plan staff time in detail to allow adequate supervision of children during transitional periods — for example, one teacher waits at the piano ready to receive children for the story after juice, while another teacher remains to clean up after juice. One teacher goes outside as soon as some children are ready.

5. Allow plenty of time. Successful transition periods require careful planning and a relaxed pace. Rushing to get from one thing to the next produces tensions and defeats the whole purpose of allowing the child greater independence and a large role in caring for his own needs and contributing to his world away from home.

6. Be clear in explaining expectations. For example, "When you get to the gym, run all the way around and then sit on the big black circle." "When you get to the room, sit on the rug." "After you put your mat away, you may take some toys to the tables," etc. Always anticipate the next situation and prepare for it.

7. Follow the same schedule each day. Offer a variety of activities within your time periods, but be consistent.

The keys to success are consistency, careful planning, organization, fairness and a sense of timing that is not so fast that you rush the children, but not so slow that they become bored or restless and begin to bug each other.

Adapted From: "Hints for Happier Transitions," by Rhoda Redleaf, Center In-Service Training Project.

The Environment

ENVIRONMENT

Space in an early childhood program enables a child to participate *actively, independently,* and *successfully.*

The minimum space requirements recommended by the National Academy of Early Childhood Programs is 35 square feet of usable indoor space and 75 square feet of enclosed outdoor space per child. Check on the licensing requirements for space in your state.

The physical space needs to be well organized with good traffic patterns and materials that are readily accessible. Children need materials that they may observe, touch or manipulate. These materials should invite investigation, imagination and spontaneous use. Children need to know where things belong and participate in maintaining the overall order.

When planning the indoor environment keep the following points in mind:

- Set up a few clearly organized centers that contain all the materials needed for each activity within each center area.

- Use low room dividers, shelves and distance to separate noisy areas from quiet ones, always making sure that all children can be observed by an adult at all times.

- Construct a permanent large motor area, such as a loft, where children may climb, jump, slide, pull themselves by their arms, wiggle and squirm.

- Provide a dramatic play area. Dramatic play and block areas provide children with opportunities to practice role playing, language skills, sharing and conflict resolution.

- Provide for individual activities as well as small group participation. For example, have one table or area for stringing beads, puzzles, small interlocking blocks, etc.

- Provide a large area for creative movement and music activities which involve the whole body.

- Set up painting easels and other "messy" activities near a source of water and on washable surfaces.

- Along with a mirror in the dramatic play area, place one above the wash basin so that children can see themselves as they wash, comb their hair and brush their teeth.

- Other things to keep in mind are: keep toileting areas totally separate from food areas; make traffic flow efficient and safe, (e.g., keeping the block area away from traffic flow) place listening center with phonograph and/or tape recorder near an outlet; place science center with plants near a light source; establish area for parents and children to check in near the door; place pictures, posters, etc., at children's eye level; have book shelves, and material shelves at children's level (except things that require supervision); have soft, private hideaways where children can get away but where staff can still observe them.

INFANT ENVIRONMENTS

The main criteria of a good infant environment are ones which encourage exploratory play, positive self-esteem, trust and mutual affection. This calls for an optimal social environment created by a caring, dedicated and skilled staff who:

- make it possible for each infant to pursue his or her own exploration of both objects and people.
- notice and give positive feedback in different ways to the infants' self-initiated explorations.
- will help passive infants to get involved in exploratory play, then encourage the infants to continue on their own.
- recognize that dressing, grooming, and washing are opportunities for promoting self-help skills, sensory experiences and attachment and, as such, are an important part of the curriculum.

Next, a good environment should:

- have distinct activity areas, e.g., diapering, sleeping, feeding, playing, staff, and a place for visiting parents.
- have play areas which are carpeted, containing a variety of soft materials for climbing over, sitting in, using as private places, etc., and are safe for children to play in with a minimum of adult interterence.
- have open play areas designed for groups of preferably about 12 infants, with traffic patterns that will not interfere with activities.
- have separate areas for children of different developmental stages (e.g., those who are still immobile, those who move by rolling, creepers and crawlers, cruisers, and walkers).
- be equipped with a variety of developmentally appropriate toys in each area, which are visible and accessible to the infants. For more mobile infants, supply low shelves from which they can choose their own activities.
- have play materials that provide a natural response to the infants exploratory actions. For instance, a baby should bang two lids together where she can see where the sound is coming from rather than play with a toy which makes a beep when a button is pushed.
- have play materials which are familiar to the infant based on past learning, yet have new features to make it challenging.

TODDLER ENVIRONMENT

The toddler environment must be a safe, healthy and stimulating one that focuses on action-based sensory experiences. It should set the stage for the toddlers' need to practice becoming autonomous, learning to interact appropriately with other children, and allow for gross motor development. It must also provide toddlers with constant opportunities to have experiences that will stretch their intellectual social, and emotional development. The room should be large, clean and cheerful with enough space to promote movement and exploration, but arranged to provide the toddler with the security of limits. Learning centers around the room work best for allowing toddlers to learn new skills and to practice old skills in their own way and at their own pace. The materials and equipment should be small enough for the toddlers to use them comfortably and unassisted. Furniture should be scaled so their legs reach the floor when seated. Clothes hooks and private cubbies should be at a height which encourages them to put their own things away without adult help.

Appropriate materials for the toddler room should be concrete and manipulative, and vary in color, size, texture, shape and complexity.

Manipulative Center

The manipulative center provides the toddler with opportunities for small motor, eye/hand coordination, and intellectual development as they begin to classify, categorize, discriminate, construct and reconstruct. Children can make choices more easily, and will sustain play with any one item longer, if fewer choices are available. The caregivers can provide variety by rotating materials on a weekly basis or as toddler(s) seem ready for a change.

- plastic snap-lock beads
- sorting boxes
- peg boards with large pegs
- bristle blocks — large
- spools to string
- small animals, people, cars, etc.
- things to unwrap and unscrew

- simple puzzles, puzzles with knobs
- shapes boxes
- magnetic shapes
- interlocking blocks
- stacking rings and nesting cups
- snap, zipper and button boards

Sensory Play Center

Through sensory play toddlers develop concepts and learn to label their experiences as they sit, stir, measure, pour, manipulate and experiment.

- a low water table (alternately used with sand, cornmeal, styro-foam, rice)
- funnels, squeeze bottles, eye droppers
- floating objects, e.g., toy boats, corks, etc.
- mixing spoons, scoops and shovels
- measuring cups and spoons
- sand wheel
- doll clothes to wash

- egg beaters
- clear flexible tubing
- sieves, strainers and basters
- dolls to bathe and shampoo

Arts and Craft Center

Safety considerations require an adult's constant supervision at this area. These activities should be provided strictly for the purpose of sensory pleasure and free expression; not for the purpose of creating a definable product. Remember, they must learn the process before they can produce a product.

- large size paper (mania, freezer wrap, construction paper, drawing paper)
- emptied and cleaned deodorant bottles filled with tempera paints
- collage material (tissue paper, old magazines, old cards, fabric scraps, etc.
- large-size crayons
- colored chalk and chalk board
- water colors and tempera paints
- playdough
- glue and paste
- cooked spaghetti, foam, pieces of straw

- blunt-edged, soft-handled scissors
- finger paints, instant pudding
- paint brushes of various sizes
- painting easel
- paper plates, napkins, wallpaper

Block Center

Toddlers begin block play by carrying, sorting and dumping blocks before they begin to build with them. Allow them to experiment as they wish. Block building will begin when they are ready.

- large hollow blocks and small floor blocks to carry and pile up
- nests of hollow blocks or boxes to pull apart and put together
- plank to use with blocks, to be raised at one or both ends, to walk on, bounce on, or jump off
- large, soft, foam blocks of different sizes
- block props such as trucks, cars, planes, boats and people

Housekeeping/Dramatic Play Center

Boys as well as girls should be encouraged to play in the housekeeping area. Toddlers learn to play cooperatively, experiment with and develop language, exercise their imaginations, develop a sense of identity and internalize the rules of their world through dramatic play.

- sink and cupboard
- table and chairs
- dolls and doll clothes
- doll high chair
- mirror (plexiglass)
- clean, empty food containers

- refrigerator
- toy food
- baby cradle and buggy
- dresser
- buckets, etc.

- stove
- pots, pans, dishes
- toy telephone(s)
- play broom and mop

- costume box with hats, purses, lunch

Dramatic play situations such as doctor's office, grocery store or school may also be set up as toddlers become more familiar with day-to-day life. The more realistic the props available for use in dramatic play the better. For example, provide real stethoscopes, empty boxes of cereal, etc.

Quiet/Reading Center

This important area should provide a space for the toddler to get away from the group alone or for a quiet time with his or her primary caregiver.

- books appropriate for age
- easy chair, rocking chair, or couch
- bean bag chairs
- interesting posters at child's eye level
- hide-away cubbies (within adult's view)

- low book shelves
- carpeted floor or area rug
- some stuffed animals and pillows

Large-Motor Center

An important area for both indoor and outdoor play, this needs to be large area away from small toys and equipment to prevent accidents. Toddlers have a great need to run, jump, climb, slide, roll and use their bodies in endless ways.

- steps and low climbing structures
- push and pull toys
- wide balance beam
- riding toys, rocking horses
- simple obstacle courses to negotiate
- tires to climb and balance on
- cartons, big boxes or laundry baskets to climb into and out of, lug, tug and push, load and unload
- low trampoline (used with adult supervision only)
- large soft balls to push, lie on or roll over
- tunnels or empty barrels to crawl through

Music Center

Toddlers love music and rhythm. Music activities foster auditory discrimination and language skills, enhance motor development, and encourage creativity and rhythmic movement.

- record player or tape recorder
- blank tapes
- a variety of music (classical, pop, folk, country western) as well as special children's records.
- instruments (bells, small drums, xylophones, tambourines, sand paper blocks, twangers)
- wooden blocks and sticks

Nature Center

Toddlers need "real" things to examine in order to learn about the real world. This area should contain only a few items at a time. If items are left for toddlers to explore at will, they must be nontoxic and too big to swallow.

- leaves
- pine cones
- rocks
- gourds
- tree bark
- ant farm
- live plants
- birds' nests
- vegetables
- sea shells
- fish tank with fish
- hamsters, gerbils, etc.,

(Live creatures must be certified healthy by a veterinarian and be kept in nonbreakable plexiglass cages or tanks.)

Common interest areas in preschool classrooms:

- Art
- Self-concept
- Math
- Prewriting
- Housekeeping
- Music
- Science/Discovery
- Language Arts/Listening
- Social Studies/Unit display
- Manipulatives/Table toys
- Contemporary living/Self help skills
- Dramatic play (Hospital, Office, Grocery, etc.)
- Books/Literature
- Sensory (Sand, Water)
- Blocks/Transportation
- Large muscle

LEARNING CENTERS/INTEREST AREAS

Draw a diagram of the learning centers set up in your program and answer the following questions:

1. Which of the above interest areas do you currently have set up in your classroom? Are there interest areas other than those listed above?

2. Are there other interest areas that you set up on a regular basis? Which ones?

   How often are they available?

3. Which interest areas are the most popular with your students? Where do the children congregate? Where do they spend the most time?

4. Which interest areas do you feel most comfortable in? Which areas do you spend the most time in? Do safety and supervision factors influence where you spend the most time? If so, how?

5. Which interest areas do the children spend the least time in? Why do you think these areas are less popular?

6. Which interest areas do you spend the least time in? Why do you spend so little time here?

_____

(Employee)   (date)

_____

(Supervisor/Mentor)   (date)

From Diane McLinn, Greater Minneapolis Day Care Association

OUTDOOR PLAY

Outside play is an important part of a child's day. It is a time for children to build motor skills, have opportunities for social interactions, enhance self-esteem and to build cognitive and language skills. The role of the adult is to ensure a outside experience. In addition, staff provide planned activities and a learning environment which enhances the total development of the child.

Children need fresh air every day. With the exception of extreme temperatures and bitter wind chill factors, outside time is an integral part of the daily schedule. Children well enough to attend the program are well enough to play outside. Fresh air helps keep children healthy. Children become unhealthy when they spend too much time enclosed indoors in dry air caused by heating systems.

Parents are responsible for providing appropriate outdoor clothing for their children. Staff need to monitor children and give reminders to keep hats and mittens on outside.

Activities

• Talk about the objects in the immediate environment.

• Pick a theme for each nature walk. Look for examples of the focus.

• Identify and question. Wear blindfolds to touch and discover. Use the five senses as a means of successfully exploring the environment.

• Search for animal clues. Have children be detectives watching for holes, nests, footprints, matted grass.

• Use balloons, rainbow streamers, parachutes and scarves for movement activities.

THE PLAYGROUND

• Equipment must be age appropriate for children's large muscle development and encourage:

balancing	pulling	throwing	crawling
lifting	skipping	climbing	swinging
pushing	riding		

• A variety of surfaces are provided such as:

| soil | hills | sand | grass |
| flat sections | hard areas for wheel toys | | |

• The outdoor area includes shade, open area and digging space.

• Children are challenged physically and socially. Children are encouraged to take turns, cooperate, share and plan together.

• The outdoor environment can simulate the indoor environment, providing a comfortable setting for art, dramatic play, science and reading areas.

• Creativity is fostered when art, carpentry, music, movement and block building are planned out-of-doors.

MAKING THE MOST OF GETTING READY TO PLAY OUTSIDE

A common complaint from staff is the amount of time it takes to get children ready to spend 10 minutes outside. Think of the time as a learning opportunity.

1. How does putting on outdoor clothing to play outside on a cold day foster the following skills:

    *   language

    *   social

    *   fine motor

    *   self help

2. Refer to the section on guidelines for transitions. What can you do to help children make a smooth transition for getting ready to play outside?

_____

(Employee)   (date)

_____

(Supervisor/Mentor)   (date)

Resources:

Harms, Thelma and Clifford, Richard, *Early Childhood Environment Rating Scale.*

Houle, Georgia Bradley, *Learning Centers for Young Children.*

Greenman, Jim, *Caring Spaces, Learning Places: Children's Environments That Work.*

Gregson, Bob, *Outrageous Outdoor Games Book.*

Miller, Karen, *Outside Play and Learning.*

PLAYGROUND IMPROVEMENT RATING SCALE

Program_____

Number of children _____Date _____

Ages of children _____Number of staff _____

Score each item: 3—outdoor play area meets this goal very well
                   2—outdoor play area needs to be improved to meet this goal
                   1—little or no evidence that outdoor play area meets this goal

(Examples of items to look for are listed in parentheses.)

ACTIVITIES AND EQUIPMENT
Range of activities:

_____1. The equipment provides appropriate and stimulating levels of difficulty for all the age groups served (infants, toddlers, preschool children, school-age children).

_____2. A variety of equipment is provided to stimulate different types of physical activity (balls, balance beams, wheel toys, swings, climbing equipment, jump ropes, ladders, planks).

_____3. Some of the equipment and materials invite cooperative play (outdoor blocks, rocking boat, dramatic play props).

_____4. Creative materials are readily available for children (clay, carpentry, paints, water, and sand).

_____5. Some of the equipment is flexible so that it can be combined in different ways by the children with adult help if necessary (planks, climbing boxes, ladders).

_____6. The climbing equipment incorporates a variety of spatial relationships (through tunnels, up or down ramps, over or under platforms).

_____7. There is a suitable place for gardening (window box, tubs with soil, garden plot).

_____8. There are enough options for the children to choose from without unreasonable competition or waiting.

Safety and health:

_____9. The equipment is substantially constructed (anchored climbing structures and swing frames).

_____10. Cushioning is provided under swings and climbing apparatus (loose sand or tanbark at least a foot deep within a containing edgeboard, rubber padding).

_____11. Swing seats are made of pliable material.

_____12. Swings are separated from areas where children run or ride wheel toys.

_____13. Protective railings prevent children from falling from high equipment.

_____14. Equipment is well maintained (no protruding nails, splinters, flaking paint, broken parts, frayed ropes).

_____15. The play area is routinely checked and maintained (trash picked up, grass mowed, good drainage).

_____16. The health hazards from animal contamination are minimized (sand box covers, fences, children wash hands after playing outdoors).

ORGANIZATION OF PLAY AREA:

_____17. The play area is well defined (fence that cannot be climbed)

_____18. There are clear pathways and enough space between areas so traffic flows well and equipment does not obstruct the movement of children.

_____19. Space and equipment are organized so that children are readily visible and easily supervised by teachers.

_____20. Different types of activity areas are separated (tricycle paths separate from swings, sand box separate from climbing area).

_____21. Open space is available for active play.

_____22. Some space encourages quiet, thoughtful play (grassy area near trees, sandbox away from traffic)

_____23. Blocks and props can be set up outdoors for dramatic play.

_____24. Art activities can be set up outdoors.

_____25. The area is easily accessible from the classroom.

_____26. The area is readily accessible to the restrooms.

_____ 27. A drinking fountain is available.
_____ 28. Accessible and sufficient storage is provided.
_____ 29. A portion of the play area is covered for use in wet weather.
_____ 30. An adequate area is sunny in cold weather.
_____ 31. An adequate area of shade is provided in hot weather.

VARIETY OF PLAY SURFACES:
_____ 32. A hard surface is available to ride wheel toys, play group games, or dance.
_____ 33. Soil, sand, and water are available for digging and mud play.
_____ 34. A grassy or carpeted area is provided.
_____ 35. Good drainage keeps all surfaces usable.

SURROUNDING ENVIRONMENT:
_____ 36. The fence creates an effective screen for the playground by blocking out unpleasant or admitting pleasant aspects of the surrounding environment. It protects children from intrusion by passers-by.
_____ 37. The setting visible from the play area is pleasant.
_____ 38. The location is relatively quiet (little noise from railroads, traffic, factories).

SUPERVISION AND USE OF PLAY AREA:
_____ 39. A sufficient number of adults supervise the children during outdoor play.
_____ 40. Responsibility for specific areas is assigned to staff to assure that the entire playground is well supervised.
_____ 41. Teachers focus their attention on and interact with the children to enhance learning and maintain safety (adults do not talk together at length or sit passively when supervising children).
_____ 42. Children are guided to use the equipment appropriately (climb on ladders instead of tables).
_____ 43. The daily schedule includes morning and afternoon active play periods for all age groups, either outdoors or in suitably equipped indoor areas.
_____ 44. The schedule for use of the play area minimizes overlap of age groups to avoid conflicts, overcrowding, and undue competition for materials.
_____ 45. Special activities are planned for and set up in the outdoor area daily (games, painting).
_____ 46. Teachers add to or rearrange large equipment at least every six months (spools, crates, tunnels).
_____ 47. Teachers encourage and assist children in rearranging small flexible equipment (ladders, planks, boxes).
_____ 48. Most of the children are constructively involved with the equipment and activities in the playground.
_____ 49. Children help clean up the area and put away equipment.

_____ **Total Score**

Reprinted with permission from the National Association for the Education of Young Children, "How Can Playgrounds Be Improved, A Rating Scale," Lovell, P. and Harms, T., _Young Children_. Vol. 40, No. 3 (March 86) © NAEYC (pp. 3-8).

Health, Safety and Nutrition

HEALTH AND SAFETY

Early Childhood programs need to provide a healthy and safe environment for young children. This section suggests policies and procedures to incorporate into a program. Your local health department is your best resource. Staff and parents need to cooperate and work together to keep children safe and healthy.

Policy and Procedures

1. Review program policies.

2. Sign up for a certified first aid class if you have not taken one in the past three years (or as your program requires).

3. Practice using the safety inspection checklist in this chapter or the one your program presently uses.

Sanitation

Toys and equipment need to be sanitized on a regular basis. This is especially important in a program which includes infants and toddlers.

Sanitizer: 1 oz. bleach to each gallon of water mixed daily and stored in pump spray bottles away from children.

Toy Safety

No-Choke Testing Tube lets you test the safety of toys (and other objects) for children under three years old by approximating the dimensions of a young child's throat. Tubes are designed by the Consumer Product Safety Commission. Most accidents happen when toys are not age appropriate.

HANDWASHING

The single issue that can be agreed upon is the importance of handwashing for staff and children in the prevention of illness and diseases. A conscientious effort on the part of all staff will keep a healthy environment for all in the early childhood setting.

1. **Purpose**

   Handwashing represents the most effective method of preventing the transfer of bacteria from the child care provider to the children, from one child to another, or from children to the child care provider.

2. **Frequent and Effective Handwashing Must Be Done**:

   A. After any toileting or diapering.

   B. Before any meals, snacks, or food preparation of any kind.

   C. After sneezing, coughing, or wiping a runny nose.

   D. Anytime hands are obviously soiled.

   E. Before the children go home.

3. **Procedure** (for 15 seconds):

   A. Standing well away from sink, turn on the water and adjust it to the desired temperature.

   B. Wet hands and wrists thoroughly, holding them downward over sink to enable the water to run toward the fingertips.

   C. Take a generous portion of soap.

   D. Scrub each hand with the other, creating as much friction as possible by interlocking the fingers and moving the hands back and forth.

   E. Rinse the hands thoroughly by holding them under the running water, with elbows higher than the hands so that the water flows downward to the fingertips. (All soap should be carefully removed to avoid roughened skin.)

   F. Dry wrists and hands with paper towels, wiping from the area of the wrists to the fingertips. Discard each towel after one motion from wrist to fingertips.

   G. Since the faucet handle is considered contaminated, turn off the water by using a dry paper towel to cover the faucet handle.

4. Liquid soaps, especially those from a dispenser, are more sanitary. Bar soaps can harbor bacteria and their use should be discouraged.

5. Soapy rags, or diaper wipes may be used to wash infants' hands. Only one rag or wipe per infant.

6. All children, the child care provider, and/or parents need to wash their hands or have them washed at regular intervals.

Reprinted with permission from Child Care Food Program, Resources for Child Caring, Inc.

IMMUNIZATION SCHEDULE

Definition of Vaccine Codes

DTP	Diphtheria and Tetanus Toxoids and Pertussis Vaccine Absorbed
Td	Tetanus and Diphtheria Toxoids Absorbed (for age 7 and older)
Polio	Trivalent Oral Polio Vaccine
MMR	Measles, Mumps, Rubella
Hib	Haemophilus Influenzae Type B Vaccine

Schedule for Infants

Age	Vaccines
2 months	DTP -1, Polio -1
4 months	DTP -2, Polio -2
6 months	DTP-3
(12 months)	(Initial TB Screening Test, repeated as required)
15 months	MMR
18 months*	DTP -4, Polio -3
18-24 months	Hib (recommended for day care)
4-6 years (school entry)	DTP -5, Polio -4
14-16 years (and at successive 10 year intervals)	Td

*These may be given at 15 months with the MMR.

Schedule for Children Not Immunized in Early Infancy (or for children behind schedule)**

Time Interval	Children Under 7	Children 7 Years or Older
First Visit	DTP -1; Polio-I, MMR (if child is 15 months. or older)	Td-1; Polio-I; MMR
2 Months Later	DTP-2; Polio-2	Td-2; Polio-2
4 Months	DTP-3	
6-12 Months later	DTP-4; Polio-3	Td-2; Polio-3
School Entry***	DTP-5; Polio-4	
Every 10 years (from date of last DPT or Td)	Td	Td

**Children whose schedule has been interrupted and who are in the process of being immunized (i.e., awaiting the next DTP or Polio dose and in the specified waiting period between doses) may remain in day care centers until the next dose is due. Those who exceed the specified waiting period between doses must be excluded.

***Not required if DTP-4 and Polio-3 were given after 4 years of age.

CARE OF THE MILDLY ILL CHILD

There is much debate in the medical world about how sick a child must be to be excluded from early childhood programs. Sick child care is cited as **the number one problem** for working parents. The program policy regarding illness needs to be clearly communicated to parents and all staff.

Medications need to be dispensed cautiously. Medications need to be stored in a area which is not accessible to children. A program has the right to refuse to dispense any medications.

Guidelines for Administering Medications

- Prescription or nonprescription medications will not be administered to the child without the written order of a physician which indicates that the medication is for that child.

- No medication, whether prescription or nonprescription, will be administered to a child without written parental authorization.

- Keep a written record of the administration, the name of the staff member administering the medication, and the name of the child.

- All medicine should be labeled with the child's name, the name of the drug and the directions for its administration. Any unused medication should be disposed of or returned to the parent(s).

- All staff who are responsible for giving medications should be trained in specific procedures by a physician or nurse.

- When parents are having a prescription filled, have them ask the pharmacist to give them a small extra labeled bottle to bring to day care.

- Keep a medicine log sheet posted where you give it to the child (e.g., on refrigerator) so you won't forget to write down the exact time and date. Put this in the child's folder after the course of medication ends.

- Be sure you have very specific instructions about how the medicine should be given (e.g., before or after meals, with a full glass of water after the medication, tilting head, etc.). Most prescription labels do not have this information.

- Learn the possible side effects of the medication and inform the parent immediately if you observe any unexpected effects. Do not give more medication without the approval of the parent or the child's physician.

- Always read what the label says about the storage; some drugs need to be refrigerated.

- **Always read the label carefully before you give any medicine; bottles often look the same.** Be sure that the child's name is on that bottle, since several children may be taking the same medicine. As an extra precaution, some centers put medication in a bag labeled with the child's name in large letters.

- Keep medicines in a locked cabinet or out of reach of children. (Don't forget medicines in the refrigerator).

- Be sure that you do not leave medicine out without adult supervision, e.g., when you answer the telephone or leave the room. Put it away first, or take it with you. A child can take an overdose in seconds.

- Never refer to medicine as "candy" or something else children like. They may try to get more of it when unsupervised.

Reprinted with permission from *Health in Day Care*, a manual for day care providers. Georgetown University Child Development Center, Washington, D.C., 1986.

Instructions for Taking a Child's Temperature

Preparation

Shake the thermometer until the mercury line is below 95°-96°F. To avoid breakage, shake over something soft.

Where to Take the Temperature

1. In children under five years of age; axillary (armpit) temperature for screening; if axillary temperature is over 99° F (37.2° C), check with a rectal temperature.
2. In children over five years of age: oral (by mouth) temperature.

Taking Axillary (Armpit) Temperatures

1. Place the tip of the thermometer in a dry armpit.
2. Close the armpit by holding the elbow against the chest for five minutes.
3. If you're uncertain about the result, recheck it with a rectal temperature. Axillary temperatures may not be reliable. Use for screening purposes only.

Taking Rectal Temperatures

1. Have the child lie stomach down on your lap.
2. Lubricate the end of the thermometer and the child's anal opening with petroleum jelly.
3. Carefully insert the thermometer about 1" (25.4 mm) but never force it.
4. Hold the child still while the thermometer is in and press the buttocks together.
5. Leave the thermometer inside the rectum for three minutes.

Taking Oral Temperatures—use only with the older preschool child

1. Be sure the child has not recently drunk a very cold or very hot drink.
2. Place the thermometer tip under the right side of the tongue.
3. Have the child hold the thermometer in place with the lips and fingers (not the teeth).
4. Have the child breathe through the nose with the mouth closed.
5. Leave the thermometer inside the mouth for 3 minutes.
6. If the child can't keep the mouth closed because the nose is blocked, take an axillary temperature.

Reading the Thermometer

Determine where the mercury line ends by turning the thermometer slightly until the line appears. If this is difficult for you, practice.

Cleaning the Thermometer

1. Wash the thermometer with cold water and soap. (Hot water will crack the glass or break the thermometer). A cracked thermometer could cut the child and should be thrown away.
2. Rinse the thermometer with cold water.
3. Dry and wipe it with rubbing alcohol.
4. Immerse in recommended bleach solution (1 part bleach, 10 parts water) and allow to air dry.
5. Shake down the thermometer and put it back into its case.

Reprinted with permission from *Health in Day Care*, a manual for day care providers. Georgetown University Child Development Center, Washington, D.C., 1986.

ILLNESS LOG

An illness log tracks contagions. Enforcing health and safety practices will reduce illness and reduce the spread of disease in early childhood programs.

Program _____

Month _____ Classroom_____

Date of Onset	Date Reported	Child/ Staff Member	Age	Description of Illness	Seen by MD?	Number of Days Absent

Draw red horizontal line to separate weeks

From Early Childhood Directors Association, 450 N. Syndicate, Suite 5, St. Paul, MN 55104

FIRST AID AND CPR

All staff in direct contact with young children need to complete a certified first aid class. The best course is geared to working with young children. At least one person with CPR training should be on site in the program at all times.

1. Check your first aid kit to be sure it is well stocked. Use the first aid kit list.

2. Fill out and post the Emergency Phone List if you do not have one.

3. Review accident log. All minor incidents are recorded and tracked to look for patterns in who is being injured, where it's happening and what time of day. Staff can use this information to take preventative measures.

4. See sample accident report for more serious injuries. This report needs to be signed by the and kept on file for insurance purposes.

First Aid Kit List

The following is a list of items which should be included in a basic home or preschool first aid kit:

- A quick-reference first aid manual (e.g., *A Sigh of Relief—The First Aid Handbook for Childhood Emergencies*)

- Note cards and pen
- Thermometer
- Flashlight
- Blunt-tip scissors
- Tweezers
- 10 2" x 2" gauze pads
- 1 roll 4" flexible gauze bandage ("Kling")
- 1 roll 1" bandage tape bandage ("Kling")
- 25 1" and 25 assorted small Band-Aids
- 2 triangular muslin bandages
- Syrup of Ipecac (at least 10 1-oz. bottles) — Check expiration dates periodically.
- In your field trip kit, coins for pay phones, soap for washing wounds, cleansing pads, synthetic "ice" packs.

- Plastic bags (for ice packs)
- Rubber gloves
- Kleenex
- Safety pins
- 10 4" x 4" gauze pads
- 1 roll 2" flexible gauze

If a child has a special health need you will want to include additional supplies in your kit; e.g. bee sting kit or benedryl for a child with a severe allergy, sugar or honey for a child with diabetes, or inhalator for a child with asthma.

Reprinted with permission from *Health in Day Care*, a manual for day care providers. Georgetown University Child Development Center, Washington, D.C., 1986.

EMERGENCY PHONE LIST

Program Name: _____

Phone number: _____

Directions to get to program location: _____

_____

_____
(e.g., 2nd floor rear of the old Washington Elementary School Bldg. at the intersection of Main and South Sts.)

Emergency Numbers:

Police: _____

Fire Dept.: _____

Ambulance: _____

Nearest Emergency Facility: _____

Important Numbers:

Poison Center: _____

Health Consultant: _____

Child Abuse Hot Line: _____

Local Department of Social Services: _____

Battered Women's Shelter: _____

Rape Crisis Center: _____

Suicide Prevention Hotline: _____

Parents Anonymous: _____

Alcoholics Anonymous: _____

Taxi: _____

(At home you should include work numbers for any adult who might need to be reached in a hurry!)

Always give this information in emergencies:

1. Name   2. Nature of Emergency   3. Telephone Number

4. Address   5. Easy Directions

6. Exact location of injured person (e.g., backyard behind parking lot)

7. Help already given

DO NOT HANG UP BEFORE THE OTHER PERSON HANGS UP

Reprinted with permission from *Health in Day Care*, a manual for day care providers. Georgetown University Child Development Center, Washington, D.C., 1986.

ACCIDENT LOG

DATE	TIME	STAFF	CHILD'S NAME	LOCATION	EQUIPMENT	NATURE OF ACCIDENT	FIRST AID PROCEDURE USED	PARENT NOTIFIED

ACCIDENT LOG

ACCIDENT REPORT
If it takes more than a kiss to comfort, document.

Name of Child: _____ Date: _____

Reported by: _____

Nature of Accident: _____

_____

_____

_____

_____

_____

Describe Injury: _____

_____

_____

_____

Place of Accident: _____

_____

Time of Accident: _____

School Equipment Involved: _____

_____

Staff Present: _____

_____

Treatment or First Aid Administered: _____

_____

_____

_____

Was this reported to parents?   Yes _____ No _____

If injury was of a serious nature, requiring hospital emergency treatment, a full written report should be attached.

Signed _____

Parent Signature _____

(PLEASE SIGN AND RETURN TO OFFICE)

From Early Childhood Directors Association, 450 N. Syndicate, Suite 5, St. Paul MN 55104

SAFETY INSPECTION

Date _____   Inspected by _____

Bathrooms

		YES	NO
1.	Is the hot water, if accessible to children, less than 120 degrees?	❏	❏
2.	Do toilets flush properly and sinks drain properly?	❏	❏
3.	Is the bathroom ventilation system working adequately?	❏	❏
4.	Are there paper towels, roller towels, or hand dryers available for the children's use?	❏	❏
5.	Do children wash their hands before meals and after toileting?	❏	❏
6.	Are the platforms used by children underneath sinks and fountains safe and sturdy?	❏	❏
7.	Is soap for washing hands available to the children?	❏	❏
8.	Is there a wastebasket available in the bathroom?	❏	❏
9.	Are the bathroom cleansers and cleaners out of reach of the children?	❏	❏
10.	Are bathroom floors washed regularly? (recommended on a daily basis)	❏	❏

Kitchen

		YES	NO
1.	Is the refrigerator clean and running at proper temperature (40 degrees F or colder)?	❏	❏
2.	Has kitchen been inspected by the health department within the last year?	❏	❏
3.	If health inspection has taken place, were all orders complied with?	❏	❏
4.	Are sinks and sink drains in good working condition?	❏	❏
5.	Is the area free of insects or rodents?	❏	❏
6.	Is freezer clean and running at proper temperature (0 degrees F or colder)?	❏	❏
7.	Are table, chairs, counters, and floors cleaned and after meals and snacks?	❏	❏
8.	Is all food brought from homes factory packaged or bakery fresh?	❏	❏
9.	Are all cleansers and cleaning materials inaccessable and out of reach of children?	❏	❏
10.	Are all foods properly stored away from any poisons, insecticides, medications?	❏	❏
11.	Are sharp knives and objects stored high and out of reach of children?	❏	❏
12.	Are tables washed before meals and snacks?	❏	❏

Review of Accident Log

		YES	NO
1.	Has the log been reviewed for any patterns or consistencies about how, when and where accidents happen in the program?	❏	❏
2.	Have accidents been handled properly and the proper first aid administered?	❏	❏
3.	Have any policies been devised to prevent reoccurring accidents?	❏	❏
4.	Have necessary changes been made as a result of a previous staff inspection?	❏	❏

Classroom Materials and Play Areas (Indoor and Outdoor)

		YES	NO
1.	Is equipment in good condition?	❏	❏
2.	Is equipment free of sharp edges, corners, or splinters?	❏	❏
3.	Is equipment secure?	❏	❏
4.	Are materials and equipment stored in a safe manner? (Items stored high are sufficiently secured; large equipment is put away securely to prevent equipment from falling on a child?)	❏	❏

Classroom Materials and Play Areas (Continued)   YES NO

5. Is the first-aid kit accessible and complete; does it contain a first-aid chart/handbook? ❑ ❑
6. Are prescribed or non-prescribed medications separate from the first-aid kit? ❑ ❑
7. Are the floors clean and free from slippery debris or materials? ❑ ❑
8. Are concrete floors tiled, carpeted or cushioned? ❑ ❑
9. Is there adequate light throughout the facility to avoid hazards? ❑ ❑
10. Are hot radiators and surfaces covered to protect children from burns? ❑ ❑
11. Have handrails remained secure? ❑ ❑
12. Are electrical sockets covered by plug protectors? ❑ ❑
13. Are there posted emergency numbers by the phone? ❑ ❑
14. Are sharp scissors, knives and hazardous materials kept out of reach or under lock? ❑ ❑
15. Are potentially hazardous equipment and materials closely supervised?
    (Example: stove, hot plate, sharp knives, poisonous plants, tools, workbench, etc.?) ❑ ❑
16. Have medications been stored properly? (Refrigerated? Out of reach of children?) ❑ ❑
17. Has the outdoor play area been adequately secured from traffic and open water? ❑ ❑
18. Whenever children swim, is there adequate supervision and lifeguards? ❑ ❑
19. According to the review of the medication log and program medication procedures, have all medications
    (prescribed and nonprescription) been administered properly? ❑ ❑
20. In reviewing previous written reports from the licensing consultant, have all items cited in the area of health
    and safety been complied with and maintained? ❑ ❑
21. Do all staff have a clear understanding of the health and safety policies of the center? ❑ ❑

Fire Safety   YES NO

1. Are flammable materials removed from the furnace room? ❑ ❑
2. Consulting the monthly fire drill log, have problems in fire evacuation been corrected? ❑ ❑
3. Have exits remained clear and free from obstruction, especially those primary and secondary exits used in
   fire evacuation? (Be sure to check cot arrangement.) ❑ ❑
4. Are there procedures for exiting out classroom windows, if necessary? ❑ ❑
5. Is the program free from excessive use of extension cords? ❑ ❑
6. If your Christmas tree has lights, is it fire resistant? ❑ ❑
7. Are fire extinguishers in working order; have they been checked within the last year? ❑ ❑
8. Do all staff know how to operate the fire extinguisher? ❑ ❑

Transportation   YES NO

1. If cars are used, do all children use age-appropriate seat belts or a safety restraints? ❑ ❑
2. Is a first-aid kit taken on field trips? ❑ ❑
3. Whenever children cross streets, is there adult supervision? ❑ ❑
4. Are children attended at times of pick-up and delivery? ❑ ❑
5. Are vehicles in proper operating condition and serviced regularly? ❑ ❑
6. Are children's emergency numbers taken on field trips or when regular transportation is provided? ❑ ❑

From Early Childhood Directors Association, 450 N. Syndicate, Suite 5, St. Paul, MN 55104

CHILD ABUSE & NEGLECT

Reporting Child Abuse and Neglect

An important factor in providing quality care to young children is to insure their health and safety by protecting them from abuse and neglect both in their home and in your care. Approximately one million children are abused or neglected annually — 2000 will die each year as a result of abuse. It can be assumed that any child in your care can be or has been a victim of child abuse. This societal problem crosses all ethnic, cultural and income groups. It occurs to girls and boys by men and women who are within or outside the family. It is children in their first three years of life who are most vulnerable to physical abuse. The role for those who work with children is to identify the problem and to responsibly react to potentially abusive situations so that children may be protected.

Child abuse occurs as a response to stress. This stress can naturally be triggered by the pressure of meeting the many needs of young children. In addition, isolation, financial strains, illness (including chemical dependency or depression), work, discrimination or lack of resources can contribute to this stress of adults who care for children. Child abuse can also result from a pattern of discipline which includes physical punishment. The highest correlate of abuse is the abuser's own experience. Many adults who abuse or neglect children have experienced similar treatment and instinctively treat children as they were treated.

To stop child abuse, the cycle of abuse must be broken so that children do not grow up to be abusing adults. Child care providers can be important in breaking this cycle through responsible reporting of suspected or identified abuse. To fulfill this role, this process needs clarification.

Who Must Report

Anyone can report child abuse and neglect. Each state has a mandatory reporting statute. In some states, child care workers are included in the group mandated to report suspected abuse and neglect, meaning that as a child care provider you report any suspected abuse or neglect. Each child care program needs to be aware of their state's mandated reporters to determine their responsibility. In some states, failure to do so may be an offense punishable by fine or imprisonment.

What Must Be Reported

Every state has laws requiring that suspected child abuse be reported. Each state also defines abuse somewhat uniquely, usually including the elements of non-accidental physical injury, neglect, sexual abuse and emotional abuse. Everyone needs to be aware and have an understanding of the definitions used by their state. As a responsible reporter only suspected abuse need be reported to the appropriate agency. It is then the agency's responsibility to determine if abuse has occurred. In most cases it will be the physical signs and behavioral characteristics of a child which will lead you to suspicion of abuse.

Why a Report Must Be Made

In addition to protecting children and complying with state laws, reporting child abuse and neglect serves other functions:

- Provides relief to families: Abuse is sometimes a "cry for help" so as to get outside people to impose limits where inner controls are not effective.

- Halts abusive behavior: The cycle of abuse is interrupted as services and education to the family are provided.

- Begins change for the family: Appropriate services can be provided after an assessment of the family situation is made.
- Provides relief to the concerned reporter. The reporter has not only fulfilled a responsibility but has given the family an opportunity to change.
- Provides statistical information: Data is needed to assess the extent of abuse so as to plan needed services for abusive families.

How to Decide to Make a Report

One fear in reporting is how to handle the delicate feelings of children and families while also dealing with your own reactions and feelings. Several basic guidelines should be considered when intervening with children and families when abuse and neglect is suspected.

- Always believe the child.
- Keep in mind that other children may be involved.
- Remember your concern for the child's safety.
- If possible, involve another professional in this process to provide support and feedback.
- Document observations, concerns and procedures followed.
- Use child protective services as a resource. Ask questions, share information and get opinions to assist in the reporting process.

How to Make a Report

Every state has at least one agency to receive reports of suspected abuse and neglect. Reports need to be made promptly to the appropriate agency. If in doubt of who to call, or if the child is in immediate danger, call the local police. Be prepared to provide specific information about what you observed, heard and were told. Names, addresses, phone numbers, and parents' names will be needed. In many cases, a written report will be requested, following an oral report.

What Happens When a Report is Made

The responsibility of child protective services is stated as follows:

- Respond promptly to reports of alleged neglect, abuse or exploitation of children to determine the validity of the report;
- Assess the damage to children resulting from neglect and abuse; Evaluate the risk of further injury to the child while in the home and whether the child should remain in the home while rehabilitative services are provided;
- Determine and identify the family problem or problems which contribute to or result in neglect or abuse;
- Evaluate the potential for treatment to correct conditions and rehabilitate the family;
- Plan a course of treatment calculated to stabilize and rehabilitate the family through services of the protective agency and the use of other appropriate community resources to meet special needs of the child and parents;
- Initiate the treatment plan and stimulate involvement of services from community resources to meet identified special needs;
- Invoke the authority of the courts where treatment potential is minimal or where there is risk if the child remains in the home.

A specific person is assigned to accomplish these tasks. Child care workers and other professionals may be requested to give further information once an investigation is underway.

Due to confidentiality and privacy laws, child protective services may not be able to give out information about the status of the family reported. Attempts should be made to obtain the allowable information. In some cases, child protective services will be able to share the agency's determination that the report was substantiated, unsubstantiated or inconclusive, and the agency's intent to provide services. When in the best interest of the child, no information will be provided.

From *Child Abuse and Neglect, The Hennepin Co. Guide for People Who Work With Children.*

Policy and Procedure for Reporting Child Abuse

The process of reporting child abuse and neglect can be complicated and stressful for child care providers. To alleviate some of the confusion, all programs should have written policy and procedures for staff. This information should be shared with parents that enroll in the program. Considerations on policy and procedures are listed:

1. A statement of the program's concern for children's health and safety.
2. Specific definitions of abuse and neglect as stated by law.
3. Legal responsibilities of child care staff in reporting abuse and neglect.
4. A list of agencies to whom reports are made.
5. Clarification of who makes reports.
6. A statement of necessary facts needed in making a report.
7. Clarification of what documentation is necessary.
8. A copy of a reporting form.
9. Internal communication needed when making a report.
10. Procedure for written reports to appropriate agencies.
11. Procedure for approaching parents.
12. Procedure for follow-up on reports made.
13. Resources for information and assistance when caring for abused and neglected children.
14. Policy and procedure for incidents of suspected abuse by a staff member.

These policies should be presented and reviewed often and can accompany staff training regarding abuse issues.

County child protective services and state human service divisions will be useful in developing policy that conforms with county procedures and state laws.

STAFF CONCERNS REGARDING ABUSE

- *What if I am wrong?*

  A child care provider who reports "suspected" abuse in good faith cannot make a "wrong" report. In most states, those who made reports in good faith are immune from civil or criminal liability.

- *What will happen to the child?*

  Each case is handled individually. Depending on the severity of the abuse and other assessments of the family a decision will be made whether to remove the child for safety reasons. In some cases, an adult may be removed from the home. In most cases, services to the family will focus on rebuilding family relationships.

- *What good is my report?*

  Child care workers often feel powerless in the process of reporting. Each report causes a disruption to an abusive situation and alerts authorities to the potentially abusive families. Sometimes the impact of your report will not show effect until much later, possibly after the child has left your care. It is important not only to look at immediate result and changes, but at long term effects a single report may have.

- *Will my report cause a parent to harm the child further?*

  This is often a concern and sometimes a problem. If this is a fear, convey this to the authorities. You make your report so they can assess this danger. In reality, there is probably more harm to be done if a report is not made. To the parent it may seem that you are condoning their treatment of the child.

- *Should I report emotional abuse or neglect?*

  If in doubt, YES. This type of abuse and neglect is difficult to substantiate, but if unreported it is likely that no change will be made in the treatment of the child. Be aware of other kinds of abuse or neglect (physical, sexual) that may be occurring with the same children. In some cases, providing education and information to the parents can be a role the child care provider and child protective services can assume.

- *What do I do to help an abused child heal?*

  Many child care providers are left with a feeling of helplessness, and powerlessness when they are to care for abused or neglected children. Responsible reporting is only one role; effective programming for the abused child is another very important role. Training resources for this information should be sought.

I am aware of the policies and procedures of the program for reporting child abuse and/or neglect. I understand if I suspect child abuse and/or neglect I am mandated to make a report. (Check your own state statutes to verify this since mandated reporting by child care workers vary from state to state.)

_____
(Employee)   (date)

_____
(Supervisor)   (date)

_____
(Trainer)   (date)

Resources:

A Sigh of Relief, Martin Greene. First aid handbook for childhood emergencies.

Developing Safety Skills with the Young Child, Diana E. Comer.

The Organic Puppet Theatre: Children's Activities in Health Awareness, Terry Louise Schultz and Linda M. Sorenson.

Those Mean Nasty Dirty Downright Disgusting but... Invisible Germs, Judith Rice.

My Doctor, Harlow Rockwell.

Child Abuse:

The Bruises Don't Always Show. Beverly Blinde, Mary Dooley Burns, Karen Kurz Reimer, Minnesota Curriculum Services, 3554 White Bear Ave., White Bear Lake, MN 55110.

Child Abuse Issues for Child Care Providers. Greater Minneapolis Day Care Association, 1628 Elliot Ave. So., Minneapolis, MN 55404.

Intervention Strategies for Abused Children. Beth Koskie and Sandra Heidemann. Available from Greater Minneapolis Day Care Association (see above for address).

Films:

Caring for Pretty Special Children.

The Preschool Abused Child (Identification and reporting).

Touch Film with Dr. Jesse Potter (Positive Touch).

Who Do I Tell? (For children).

NUTRITION

Healthy and well balanced meals and snacks will provide a child with the energy needed to grow and develop to his or her potential. Life long habits are established in the early years. Teachers of young children need to reinforce good eating habits by providing balanced food choice and by incorporating nutrition education into the curriculum.

1. Review today's menu to see if it meets the Child Care Food Program requirements.

2. Design a lesson plan with a theme centered on a nutrition issue. Include art activities, literature, songs, fingerplays and movement.

FOODS TO AVOID FOR INFANTS AND TODDLERS

Some foods are not readily digestible and/or can cause choking. The following foods are:

Not Recommended for Children Under 16 Months:

Not Readily Digestible	Chokable
• Bacon*	• Bread sticks
• Baked beans*	• Candy
• Corn*	• Raw carrots*
• Raw cucumber	• Raw celery*
• Leafy vegetables	• Peeling on fruit*
• Raw onion*	• Things with seeds
• Raisins*	• Nuts*
• Bran*	• Olives*
• Heavily spiced foods*	• Chunky peanut butter*
• Chocolate	• Pizza*
	• Popcorn*
	• Hot dogs unless diced*

*Not recommended for young toddlers 16-24 months

Not Recommended for Children Under 12 Months:

• Beets   • Spinach   • Melon   • Berries

Resources:

Super Snacks for Kids, Penny Warner.

Recipes to Grow On, Central Minnesota Child Care Inc.

More Than Graham Crackers, Nancy Wanamaker, et.al.

Learning Through Cooking: A Cooking Program for Children Two to Ten, Nancy J. Ferreira.

Learning from Cooking Experiences, Thelma Harms.

FOOD CHART

Child Care Food Program

	Ages 1-3	Ages 3-6
BREAKFAST		
Milk	1/2 cup	3/4 cup
Juice or Fruit or Vegetable	1/4 cup	1/2 cup
Bread or	1/2 slice	1/2 slice
Cereal	1/4 cup	1/3 cup
SNACK		
Milk or		
Juice or Fruit or Vegetable	1/2 cup	1/2 cup
Bread or	1/2 slice	1/2 slice
Cereal	1/4 cup	1/3 cup
LUNCH/SUPPER		
Milk	1/2 cup	3/4 cup
Meat or Poultry or Fish or	1 ounce	1-1/2 oz.
Cheese or	1 ounce	1-1/2 oz.
Eggs or	1	1
Peanut Butter or	2 Tablespoons	3 Tablespoons
Dried Beans and Peas	1/4 cup	3/8 cup
Fruits (2 or more) or		
Vegetables (2 or more) or		
Fruits&Vegetables to total	1/2 cup	1 cup
Bread	1/2 slice	1/2 slice

Recordkeeping:
- Keep menu records
- Count meals served:
  - to enrolled children
  - to adult staff
  - to other adults

Points to Remember:
- Use fluid milk
- Use bread or cereal made from enriched or whole grain flour
- Use full-strength milk and juice
- Each child must be served the required amount of each food group at all meals.

Reprinted with permission from *Health in Day Care*, a manual for day care providers, Georgetown University Child Development Center, Washington, D.C., 1986.

Team Building

TEAM BUILDING

You are part of a team whose goal is to provide a quality experience for the children in your care. A team working cooperatively can consistently provide a better experience than individual members working alone. As a member of a team, you benefit from others' ideas and efforts to offer a more creative program. Each team member differs in experience, interests, strengths and weaknesses. All members have the opportunity to grow and develop in understanding and ability. Learning to work together takes time, patience, mutual understanding, willingness to persevere and a good sense of humor. The quality of a child care program is determined by the quality of the staff. An effective child care team provides:

- Friends and colleagues who are caring, supportive and appreciative.
- Opportunities to be useful, challenged and praised.
- Involvement in decision making about things which directly affects them.

CREATIVE PROBLEM SOLVING

Creative problem solving focuses on involving everyone. Use the creative problem solving with a team you are working with. Begin by using the case studies for practice. Then use the model for a problem you are currently concerned about. The creative problem solving can be used for any concern requiring decision making. team members can use it as a guide for dealing with staff relations, how to handle difficult behavior with a particular child or a parent concern. This model works best with a maximum of seven people. And remember, two heads work better than one.

Case Studies

1. Patty is friendly and talkative one day and the next day she'll only speak curtly when spoken to. Several staff have asked her if anything is wrong. Her answer is "Nothing." Is this a problem?

2. Laurie and Sandy open up the center at 7:00 a.m. Laurie lives one block from the center and walks to work. Sandy commutes 10 miles on a busy freeway and is often at least 10 minutes late for work. Is this a problem?

3. Linda is the head teacher in the three-year-old room. Susie is her assistant. They also are roommates. Susie has recently taken a second job at night as a waitress. She spends nap time with the children sleeping. Is this a problem?

4. Alice is a single mother. She is waiting at the door, with her daughter in pajamas, when Laurie arrives in the morning to open the center. Alice smiles sweetly as she passes her daughter, Jessica, over to Laurie after Laurie unlocks the door. As Alice runs down the walk she yells, "I hope you don't mind, but I'm going to be late again and my boss will kill me." Is this a problem?

5. Mary and Betsey work in the infant room. Betsey has sprained her wrist and cannot lift anything (or anybody) over 10 lbs. for six weeks. Is this a problem?

6. Leslie sits in staff meetings with her arms folded or else doodles on a sheet of paper. She avoids all contact and does not enter in on any conversations. When directly asked for an opinion she states that she doesn't care or else doesn't know. Is this a problem?

7. State the problem your team is currently concerned about.

Creative Problem Solving Example

Patty is friendly and talkative one day and the next day she'll only speak curtly when spoken to. Several staff have asked her if anything is wrong. Her answer is "Nothing."

1. **What is the problem?**
   Patty's mood swings and the affect they have on the staff she works with.
   What else do I need to know?
   Who is involved: People Patty has contact with: staff, parents and children.
   What happens: Staff avoids involvement or confrontations.
   Where does this happen: In the classroom.
   How often: Several times a week.
   When: Unpredictable.

2. **What is the real problem?**
   Creates staff tension.
   What is my basic objective? To open communication lines with Patty and the rest of the staff to work as an effective team.

3. **Ideas: Brainstorm without censoring.**
   Fire Patty.
   Director confronts Patty.
   Team Leader confronts Patty.
   Ignore her completely.
   Give her a pin to wear when she's having a bad day so staff will be warned and not feel responsible.

4. **Solution**: Staff working with Patty share in a kind and caring way their concern about the tension caused by her mood swings.
   Advantages:
   • Open and direct method.
   • Patty may explain reasons for her moods and staff may be able to help.
   • Builds feeling as a team and sets up a method to deal with future problems.
   • Staff will probably find out that Patty's moods have nothing to do with them.
   • Patty may decide to seek counseling.
   Disadvantages:
   • Patty may feel threatened.
   • Patty may become defensive.

   By confronting Patty, action takes place and the problem will be brought out in the open to release tension felt by Patty's co-workers.

5. **Acceptance**:
   Ways to implement: Staff will agree to confront Patty when she is in "one of her moods." Patty will agree to acknowledge it and let staff know how they can help.
   Who might help: The director may serve as a mediator or bring in an outside consultant who can facilitate the group meeting.
   Time: This plan will be implemented for two weeks.
   Places: In the classroom.
   New Challenges Posed: Assertiveness training may be necessary for all staff.

6. **Evaluation**:
   After two weeks the original group will sit down and review the situation. Improvements will be noted, congratulations to all to keep up the work. If the problem still exists with no improvement a new solution from the brainstorming session will be implemented.

TEAMBUILDING

Creative Problem Solving

1. What is the problem?

    a. What else do I need to know: Who, What, Where, How, When

    b. Where are the answers?

2. What is the real problem? What is my basic objective?

3. Ideas: BRAINSTORM

4. Solution: Advantages and Disadvantages

5. Acceptance: Ways to Implement

    Who might help

    Time

    Places

    New Challenges Posed

6. Evaluation

TEAM RELATIONS

Open communication fosters team building. Staff need to treat each other with the same respect with which they treat children. Conflicts are part of human nature. Conflicts themselves are not the culprit of destroying team relations as much as the way the conflict is treated by those involved. Think of a situation when you may have used each of the following problem solving styles. What was the result?

1. Avoidance — "If I ignore it, it will go away."
    By procrastinating or ignoring a problem, hope that it will go away or someone else will take care of it.

2. Authorization — "Because I said so."
    One person makes the decision for all the people involved.

3. Permissive — "Whatever you say."
    No opinions or suggestions are offered, allowing the other person to dominate.

4. Creative Problem Solving — "The more ideas, the better the solution." Everyone is involved in decision making.

_____   _____
(Employee)   (date)

_____   _____
(Supervisor/Mentor)   (date)

TEAM BUILDING EXERCISE

1. List responsibilities and tasks that each member of your team shares: (e.g., room environment, snack preparation)

2. The advantages of working as a team outweigh the disadvantages. However, as part of a team, conflicts and problems can arise. List specific examples of problems based on your own professional and/or personal experience for the issues below. Write examples of how these problems can be prevented.

    • Arranging time for planning

    • Differing attitudes and values

    • Individual perceptions

    • Resistance to change

3. What are your strengths? What can you contribute as a member of your team?

4. What would you like to learn from your team members?

_____

(Employee)   (date)

_____

(Supervisor/Mentor)   (date)

COMMUNICATION SKILLS

In our relationship with staff as well as with children and their parents, developing good communication skills is essential.

Carl Rogers, a noted psychologist, has coined the phrase "active" listening. It is often difficult to silence our inner voice which is often preparing a response before the person we are listening to has completed a sentence. Active listening allows us to focus on the other person's feelings, asking questions only to clarify or to encourage the other person to express more. The following active listening techniques are explained in Rogers' book, *Becoming a Person*.

Active Listening Skills

1. Parroting: Tell the person, as exactly as you can, what you heard her say.
   Speaker: "I feel sad."
   You: "You feel sad."
   As simple as this is, parroting is an effective way to let a person know you "hear" and to encourage further expression.

2. Paraphrasing: Rephrase what you heard in your own words.
   Speaker: "I don't like you."
   You: "You feel mad at me."

3. Ask clarifying questions.
   Speaker: "I don't want to go home."
   You: "Can you tell me why you are upset about going home today."

4. Use nonverbal cues indicating interest and understanding (eye contact, body posture, nodding your head).

Active Listening

Think about your reactions when in a conversation with another person. Do you:

- Respond to what the person has said or switch the topic to something you are interested in? Think how you would feel if you came to work excited about the litter of kittens your cat just had and your co-worker commented on the weather. You will be surprised how often this happens.

- Pick up on the speaker's statements but direct the conversation towards yourself? In response to your news about a litter of kittens, your co-worker would talk about her pet. This is the most common response level in casual conversation.

- Ask for additional information and focus on the persons feelings? Your co-worker would ask you how many kittens are in the litter, what color are they, etc., and if you are happy or sad since you may have to give them away.

ACTIVE LISTENING

Exercise 1:

Intentionally use active listening responses for a day. Record general responses. What did you discover?

Exercise 2:

Instructions: Find a partner to present a problem. Do not try to solve the problem or offer advice. Use active listening skills to explore the problem and encourage your partner to think of his or her own solution. Practice 5 minutes and record response.

_____

(Employee)   (date)

_____

(Supervisor/Mentor)   (date)

NONVERBAL COMMUNICATION

Research indicates that over 50% of our communication is nonverbal. Nonverbal communication is even more significant in working with young children who are just beginning to master verbal communication. They lack the skills needed to express their needs verbally. We need to be sensitive to the nonverbal cues children give us. In addition, we need to be aware of how sensitive children are to the nonverbal cues we give.

How a person expresses or hides emotions nonverbally is determined by a combination of factors. People from different countries or from different racial or ethnic groups within one country may express different nonverbal communication. When people from different cultural backgrounds encounter each other they may miscommunicate because of these differing nonverbal communication patterns. Also, how a person communicates nonverbally depends on peer groups, past experience and training or conditioning. Therefore, nonverbal cues may be viewed as indicators. Comprehensive understanding depends on agreement between verbal and nonverbal cues. Mixed messages are a contradiction between verbal and nonverbal cues.

List nonverbal characteristics that indicate the following emotions:

EMOTION	FACIAL EXPRESSIONS eyes/mouth	POSTURE arms/hands/legs/feet/ head/shoulders	VOICE TONE
joy			
anger			
sadness			
confusion			
boredom			

Note: As an adult, be aware of the importance of communicating with a child at his or her eye level. If your knees are weak, make sure a low chair is close by. Think of someone constantly talking over your head!

A TIME FOR REFLECTION

Think about the following questions. Periodically, come back and review them. As a team member you have as much responsibility as anyone else to keep the team productive, healthy and happy.

1. Are team members caring, supporting and appreciative of each other?

2. Does the team feel useful, challenged and recognized for work well done?

3. Are all members involved in decision making when appropriate?

4. Are the group goals clear?

5. Does the group listen to each other?

As a team, consider some things that can be done to improve team relations.

Taking Care of Yourself

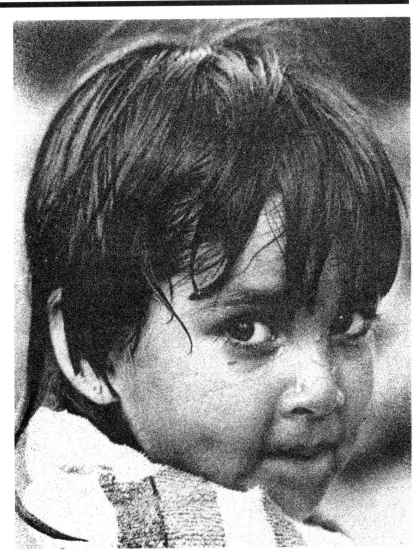

GETTING IN TOUCH WITH YOURSELF

As a role model for young children, you need to feel good about yourself. This activity can be used at a staff meeting or shared with your mentor or supervisor.

1. Why did you choose to work with young children?

2. What benefits will your position bring to your own personal growth and development?

3. Why is your job so important?

4. List the special qualities you have that make you a good teacher.

5. What support do you need from your co-workers and supervisor to help meet your needs?

SELF-ESTEEM

One of the most important aspects of your position as a teacher is to help young children build a healthy and positive self- esteem. In order to do this, you must feel good about yourself. We tend to be our harshest critics. We need to reprogram our negative self-talk in order to create the positive energy we need to fulfill our own potential.

Choose a word to represent each letter in your name to describe the "you" which you want to be and *can* be.

Example: JANICE

     Jubilant
     Active
     Novel
     Independent
     Creative
     Expressive

Continue to add words. Use a dictionary for more constructive and positive words to describe you.

AVOIDING BURNOUT

Working with young children is a rewarding and challenging job. However, people working with young children sometimes feel that the importance of their job is not recognized by parents, supervisors or by society in general. Frustrations also occurs from working with difficult children and not seeing progress, lack of resources, materials and equipment, conflict and lack of feedback from supervisors and co-workers and low wages.

AVOIDING BURNOUT

A healthy work environment provides you with the support needed to overcome the obstacles encountered in your job. Talk to your supervisor about concerns or problems you may identify when completing the following statements.

I get recognition for my job from.....

My job fulfills my needs and interests by

My skills and talents used in my job are.....

_____   _____
(Employee)   (date)

_____   _____
(Supervisor/Mentor)   (date)

PERSONAL TIME

A happy, healthy and functional person has an active and well rounded lifestyle. Using the scale below, rate your satisfaction concerning the role of the following factors in your life.

PERSONAL TIME

1	3	5
Low		High
Satisfaction		Satisfaction

____ Exercise   ____ Hobbies, Interests
____ Diet   ____ Relationships
____ Relaxation   ____ Time Management

- Identify areas you would like to improve.

- List for each area the results/goals you want to accomplish.

- Write down specific action or steps you will take to accomplish this goal.

- For each action or step, specify your time frame.

- List the resources you will need. Include people, materials, money.

- Set up evaluation checkpoints.

TIME MANAGEMENT TIPS

- Plan and record lesson plans weekly.
- Use one calendar to chart birthdays, field trips, special events, date return for library books, information due for newsletter and so on.
- Use log system to leave notes for parents and staff.
- Post daily schedule, lesson plans, parent's names, substitutes, children's allergies, etc.
- Send parents reminders about conferences, field trips and other events.
- Use graphic symbols to make it easier for children to put things away.
- Organize work area.
- Schedule routine tasks.
- Accept and return telephone calls during a specified time of day.
- Schedule evaluation and feedback sessions with supervisor.

Resources:

Avoiding Burnout, Paula Jorde Bloom.

Evaluation and Training Plan

EVALUATION AND TRAINING

Program Evaluation

The National Academy of Early Childhood Programs' Accreditation system ranks program evaluation as an important component of a high quality early childhood program. Assessment of goals for children, staff and parents helps a program maintain and improve standards for the quality of care and education of young children. The self-study materials provided by the Academy are:

- classroom observation tool
- parent questionnaire
- staff questionnaire
- administrator's report

These tools help a program evaluate criteria in ten areas:

- Interaction among staff and children
- Curriculum
- Staff - parent interaction
- Staff qualifications and development
- Administration
- Staffing
- Physical environment
- Health and safety
- Nutrition and food service
- Evaluation

For more information about Accreditation call NAEYC at 800-424-2460.

Self Evaluation

This manual has been designed to actively involve you in the orientation process. The more we find out, the more there seems to be to learn and to know. The challenge and the benefit of working with young children is that we continue in our own growth and development.

This manual has been designed to give an opportunity for feedback. Evaluations provide the necessary feedback needed to continue to improve in our jobs.

We all feel good when someone else tells us how well we do our jobs. However, the most important person to please is ourselves. The most meaningful evaluation starts from our own assessment of our:

- Strengths
- Areas to improve
- Progress
- Future goals

Based on the overview of the material in this manual complete the following training plan. A special thanks to you for choosing to do this important work of caring for our children — our most important investment in the future.

EVALUATION AND TRAINING PLAN

- My strengths as a teacher of young children are:

- Areas in which I wish to improve are:

- Specific areas of needs are:

- Learning experiences and resources to be used:

- Action plan: write in specific goals, action, timeline:

- Date of follow-up conference with my supervisor:

_____
(Employee)   (date)

_____
(Supervisor/Mentor)   (date)

OTHER TOYS 'N THINGS PRESS PUBLICATIONS

All Season Fun & Frolic — Indoor and outdoor activities for toddlers to school age.

Basic Guide to Family Day Care Record Keeping — Clear instructions on keeping necessary family day care business records.

Calendar-Keeper — Activities, family day care record keeping, recipes and more. Updated annually. Most popular publication in the field.

Child Care Resource & Referral Counselors & Trainers Manual — Both a ready reference for the busy phone counselor and a training guide for resource and referral agencies.

The Dynamic Infant — Combines an overview of child development with innovative movement and sensory experiences for infants and toddlers.

Family Day Caring magazine — The best source of information on every aspect of home-based child care.

Family Day Care Tax Workbook — Updated every year, latest step-by-step information on forms, depreciation, etc.

For You, For Them — Trainer bibliography of audio-visual and print resources in 6 topic areas.

Forms Kit for Directors — Over 150 reproducible forms covering every need in an early childhood program.

Heart to Heart Caregiving: A Sourcebook of Family Day Care Activities, Projects and Practical Provider Support — Excellent ideas and guidance written by an experienced provider.

Kids Encyclopedia of Things to Make and Do — Nearly 2,000 art and craft projects for children aged 4-10.

Open the Door, Let's Explore — Full of fun, inexpensive neighborhood walks and field trips designed to help young children.

S.O.S. Kit for Directors — Offers range of brainstormed solutions to everyday questions and problems.

Sharing in the Caring — Packets with family day care parent brochure, contracts and hints.

Survival Kit for Early Childhood Directors — Solutions, implementation steps and results to handling difficulties with children, staff, parents.

Teachables From Trashables — Step-by-step guide to making over 50 fun toys from recycled household junk.

Teachables II — Similar to above; with another 75-plus toys.

Those Mean Nasty Dirty Downright Disgusting but... Invisible Germs — A delightful story that reinforces for children the benefits of frequent hand washing.